MONTANA
WEEKENDER
ROAD TRIPS

PUBLISHED BY

FACING PAGE TOP: *Flathead Lake's northwest corner*
RICK & SUSIE GRAETZ PHOTO

FACING PAGE BOTTOM: *Ready to run at Showdown*
RICK AND SUSIE GRAETZ PHOTO

PRECEDING PAGE: *Autumn colors in the mountains of northwestern Montana*
JOHN LAMBING PHOTO

COVER, MAIN PHOTO: *Summertime pleasures of the Gallatin Mountains*
JOHN REDDY PHOTO

INSET, LEFT: *Virginia City*
SCOTT WHEELER PHOTO

INSET, CENTER: *Sandhill crane*
DONALD M. PHOTO

INSET, RIGHT: *Red Lodge Ski Area*
RICK GRAETZ PHOTO

ISBN I-56037-I36-6

For more information on our books write: Montana Magazine,
P.O. Box 5630, Helena, MT 59604 or call: (800) 654-1105.
www.montanamagazine.com

Printed in Korea

CONTENTS

SPRING

Ski, Snow, & Soak

by Don Snow

I T'S FUNNY WHAT YOU THINK ABOUT, SOAKING IN HOT MINERAL WATER WHILE FROST FORMS ON YOUR HEAD. Sitting under a spigot in the hot end of the pool at Jackson Hot Springs Lodge, I had a phrase running through my head—a phrase taken from a sign I saw on the doorway of an antique store in this very town four years ago. The sign read, "Monica Vaquera's Independent Order of Optimistic Females." I remember it, because I saw it the first time I brought my Southern bride to this little village at the high end of the Big Hole Valley.

Fourth of July, 1992, we rode through town on bicycles just in time for the Jackson Independence Day celebration. My wife Dorothy, a strict vegetarian in those days, was new to Montana, and we were both new to two-wheel road trips. As we coursed smoothly through the festive main drag of Jackson, a fellow with a big cowboy hat turned from his streetside barbecue grill and pushed a long fork our way. From the end dangled a strip of juicy beef, sizzling with a blackened sauce. Without even touching her brakes, my vegetarian sweetheart grabbed that thing in her teeth and just kept riding. I could see her jaws working hard as we stopped a couple of blocks later to read the enigmatic insignia of one Monica Vaquera. Desirous only of the open road, we quickly made our way out of town without ever finding out what an "Independent Order of Optimistic Females" might amount to. These days, no one seems to remember.

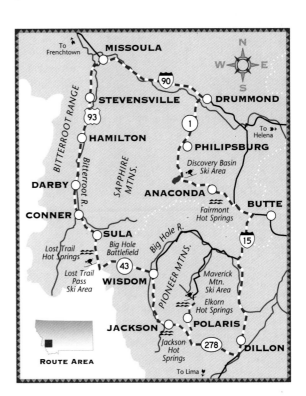

FACING PAGE: *The Big Hole Valley*
RICK GRAETZ PHOTO

PRECEDING PAGE: *Carter Pond at the base of the Judith Mountains*
GEORGE WUERTHNER PHOTO

WELCOME TO THE BIG HOLE

There's something about this high valley, often the coldest spot in the lower 48, that makes you just want to join right in. Maybe it's the people—friendly and warm enough to drive away the chill, at least every time I've been up here, and I come a lot, fishing, biking, hiking, or just driving around. This time I was here for the skiing and the hot springs, the best combination I know of to cast off that winter deep freeze.

GETTING TO LOST

I lived in the Bitterroot Valley for ten years, and know enough to start our ski-'n'-soak adventure in Hamilton with an official trip-launch breakfast at the Coffee Cup Cafe. Then it was on to the Ravalli County Museum, located in the former county courthouse on the corner of South 3rd and Bedford. It must be one of the finest county museums in the state. I'm especially fond of its chronicle of Hamilton's Rocky Mountain Laboratory, originally

Elkhorn Hot Springs
DON SNOW PHOTO

a wood tick disease lab where researchers tried to find a cure for Rocky Mountain spotted fever.

The Marcus Daly Mansion on the Eastside Highway runs its tours between April 15 and October 15. For five bucks, you can get a glimpse of how the copper barons lived. A friend once called it "Tara, Montana"—twenty-four bedrooms, fifteen baths, and seven fireplaces, most of them chiselled from Italian marble. On Memorial Day weekend, the Daly Mansion conducts its annual doll show.

Out of Hamilton we headed straightaway for Lost Trail Hot Springs about four miles south of Sula (check out the unexpected collection of fine Western clothing and Indian jewelry at the Sula Store). On the way up U.S. Highway 93, we stopped in at the Camp Creek Inn to get the skinny on the Lost Trail Ski Area. Bill Grasser, who has owned and operated Lost Trail for thirty years, also owns Camp Creek, a beautiful ranchhouse bed and breakfast with buildings dating to 1920. Set a few hundred yards back from the highway, the spacious main house offers three upstairs guest rooms, plus there's a pair of cabins. Camp Creek is a great base for families or couples who ski downhill at Lost Trail or cross-country ski on nearby Chief Joseph Pass.

Ranch manager Sandy Skorupa loves to talk history, and showed us a photo collection of the original ranch crew, mostly members of the Gallogly family.

Originally dubbed the Pine Knot Ranch, this may have been a house built by hair tonic. Two of the original owners, Uncle Jim and Elmer Gallogly, were in business—or maybe just cahoots—with Mr. Newbro, who owned Newbro Drugs in Butte. Elmer, a pharmacist, came up with the formula for the highly successful Newbro Hair Herpicide which

GREAT CROSS-COUNTRY SKI TRAILS (EASY TO EXPERT) TAKE OFF FROM CHIEF JOSEPH PASS

"Makes a Balding Head Lush and Thick."

Sandy left us to ponder the meaning of the word "herpicide" (snake killer? Do snakes cause baldness? I thought it was one's mother's genes.) while she bounced over to the dining room window and pointed to a beautiful old bell hanging from a tower next to the tack shed. "From Detroit," she announced. "Came from a schoolhouse where Henry Ford went to school."

Those Galloglys got around.

Aunt Polly Gallogly, pictured in a flat straw hat with a ribbon, was a schoolteacher whose students included Zane Grey. Years later, Zane stayed at the Pine Knot while working on his novel *Thunder Mountain*.

Sandy filled us in on the major expansion planned for the ski hill. The new Saddle Mountain extension, to be built over the next five years, will include two new lifts, at least a dozen runs, and a new lodge. It will add 600 feet to the current vertical rise of 1,200 feet.

Bill Grasser manages to keep his prices low, and according to Sandy, that tradition will continue even after the expansion. "Bill's committed to a place where the average person can afford to ski," she said. The platinum crowd, according to Bill, need not apply.

Back on the road, we topped Chief Joseph Pass at 7,264 feet along State Highway 43. Excellent cross-country ski trails take off on both sides of the highway, and there's good parking. The weekly maintenance of these trails is a labor of love for Gordon Reese of Corvallis and the 65-member Bitterroot Cross Country Ski Club. They groom thirteen trails in all, most of them running about a mile in length and ranging in difficulty from easy to expert. Maps of the ski trails can be obtained from the ski club, and they wouldn't object if skiers who enjoy the trails and cabins would send $10 club memberships ($20 for families) to Box 431, Corvallis, 59828.

Skiers can reserve either the May Creek or Hogan Cabin for overnight ski-in-and-stays. These Forest Service cabins are each equipped with a propane cook stove and plenty of firewood. The cabins can be reserved by calling the Forest Service at 689-3243, beginning around October 15. If you're interested, call early.

GAINING WISDOM

Montana poet Richard Hugo once asked in one of his famous drinking-and-driving poems, "Why name a town Wisdom?" Carol Sperling, the ranger on duty at the Big Hole Battlefield Visitor's Center, had the answer. She reminded us that Lewis and Clark named today's Big Hole, Beaverhead, and Ruby rivers the Wisdom, Philosophy, and Philanthropy rivers, in honor of President Jefferson's favorite virtues. The virtues didn't stick to the rivers, but the name Wisdom stuck to the town that lies in the middle of the Big Hole Valley.

The Big Hole Battlefield, site of the August 1877 attack by the U.S.

Tipi poles at the Big Hole Battlefield
SCOTT WHEELER PHOTO

cavalry on the Nez Perce, remains open all winter. "The road down to the battlefield parking lot doesn't get plowed, but you can still go there," Sperling said. "The skiing is great," she added, but then admitted, "I'm pretty much the only one who skis down there. At thirty-five–below you don't want to stay out too long."

At Wisdom in time for a late lunch, we flipped a coin to settle the debate between Fetty's (established in 1932), and the new upstart, the Big Hole Crossroads Restaurant. We like both, but this trip, the Crossroads won the toss. The steak sandwiches are excellent, and I even enjoy the coffee—one of the real weaknesses of many other Montana home-cooking establishments.

On the highway, the debate began among us three wannabe hot-pot connoisseurs: Dorothy, my twelve-year-old daughter Tenly, and me. The choices this trip were among Lost Trail, Jackson, Elkhorn, and Fairmont hot springs, all of them in perfect spots for ski-'n'-soaks. We each got two votes.

Lost Trail Hot Springs is an older resort, with rustic cabins, a full service bar, and handsome restaurant. It lies along U.S. 93 at the foot of Lost Trail Pass. This one got an immediate vote from Tenly. The big swimming pool is warm, not hot, so she could cavort for an hour or more without boiling over. A true Montana girl, this kid has a low tolerance for heat.

Dorothy and I, meanwhile, stayed inside the covered hot tub, away from the pool and pleasantly surrounded with potted plants. When two other couples showed up, things got a bit crowded, but we didn't mind. The water runs warm enough to make me sweat, and that's what I came for.

For my money—and there's not much of it—Jackson Hot Springs is one of Montana's treasures. The cavernous main lodge feels warm and nicely lighted—not always the case inside older log structures. The bar is open and inviting, and although a few poker machines line one wall, they don't rule the place.

Owners Monte and Inge Peterson run a tight ship here. The food, strongly influenced by Inge's German background, is excellent. Plus there's a decent wine list and a slew of imported and micro beers to go with it. We've stayed in the cabins several times and have always found them clean, cheerful, and warm. Best of all, the outdoor pool is nice and hot, with plenty of spigots lining the sides. This one got votes from Dorothy and me, while Tenly lay gasping onshore.

Polaris
DON SNOW PHOTO

ON TO POLARIS

Elkhorn Hot Springs resort lies at the upper reaches of Grasshopper Creek, just four miles or so from Maverick Mountain Ski Area (above the metropolis of Polaris). The dirt washboard into Polaris winds through the historic Tash Ranch and past the lovely Polaris School, in continuous operation since 1892. I was dismayed to find the Polar Bar, a one-table roadside classic, closed on the afternoon we dropped by, but Maverick Mountain was running strong. With nearly 2,000 feet of vertical rise and average annual snowfalls of 200 inches, Maverick offers some dyne-o-mite downhill runs, including a pair of homologated race courses. "Homologated" means officially approved by the moguls of international skiing. (Sure, but have they ever used hair herpicide?)

Elkhorn sits in one of the snowiest little basins in southwest Montana. The first time I stayed at the resort—maybe seventeen years ago—I remember being impressed at its extreme rusticity. You can measure rusticity by the amount of light that can be seen through the gaps between the logs of your sleeping cabin, and mine had gaps wide enough to poke a carbine through and collect an elk.

Well, a lot has changed there.

A half-dozen new cabins have been built, and several of the oldsters have been improved. The main attraction in the central lodge is still a cozy, folksy dining room that features home-cookin' and numerous taxidermy mounts that gaze with glassy serenity from the tall log walls. The springs are much as I remember them: a pair of outdoor pools, one much larger than the other, and an indoor "wet sauna" brimming with steam and wonderfully hot water (about 110 degrees, which is a lot hotter than it sounds). One of the great treats at Elkhorn is the upper body massage you can give yourself simply by sitting underneath the overflow pipe connecting the outdoor pools, where a wrist-thick stream plunges several feet into the smaller pool. It takes an old Finn-lander like me and knocks him happily senseless. One more vote is cast, from the melting snowman.

The cross-country skiing at Elkhorn is just plain fabulous. At over 7,000 feet in elevation, most years the snow lasts well into spring. Owner Patty Lovaas said that over thirty miles of groomed trails wander from the resort up into the Pioneer Mountains, with another 150 miles of snowmobile trails. The Lovaas family rents cross-country equipment and snowmobiles, so first-timers can just show up and give it a try.

DISCOVERING FAIRMONT

Be sure to visit the Patagonia Outlet Store on North Idaho Street in Dillon. I used to sneer at New West clothing—"tofu underwear"—until I started using it, then bigotry caved in to practicality. This store has the best bargains on the best clothes in North America.

Also, check out the Beaverhead County Museum next to the railroad tracks downtown—an excellent collection of early ranch-life artifacts. The Lion's Den Restaurant, located next to the I-15 interchange north of town, serves generous portions. I've had decent halibut there, and on a different trip, a slice of prime rib the size of a snowshoe.

Road question: if Wise River had a high school, would its football team be known as the Fighting Wise Guys? Our query was met with the blank stares it deserved, at the Wise River Inn, so we got out of town fast and

DISCOVERY BASIN HAS STEEP LITTLE BASINS OFTEN BRIMMING WITH CHAMPAGNE POWDER

looped on over to another chance to ski-'n'-soak.

Discovery Basin Ski Area, about thirty miles west of Anaconda, is two ski areas in one. The original face offers very good intermediate and beginner skiing on two dozen slopes and trails. But don't let the relatively modest vertical drop of 1,300 feet fool you. The new "Backside" of the mountain is mostly for experts—its steep little basins are often brimming with champagne powder.

Afterwards you can head for Fairmont Hot Springs, unquestionably the largest and most modern hot springs resort in Montana. This one notched another enthusiastic vote from Tenly, who couldn't get enough of the waterslide.

Back to Missoula and its well known attractions, we settle in at home. On reflection, we realize what an incredible circuit we've made. With four hot springs resorts, each a local call away from three good downhill basins, plus innumerable opportunities for cross-country and snowshoeing, these mountains of southwest Montana offer a wintertime paradise. Once the ice breaks on the Big Hole, we'll be back with rods, rafts, and bicycles (our only shuttle vehicles), for another chance at gaining Wisdom. ✧

Trout, Trails, & Tours

by Carmen Winslow

IN MARCH THE SNOW BEGINS TO SOFTEN AND THE DAYLIGHT LENGTHENS. IT'S THE "IN-BETWEEN SEASON"—unpredictable weather, spring snowstorms erupting out of nowhere, and temperatures dropping or rising with no warning.

The key is preparation, and any spring outing requires the same gear as a winter adventure. You may not have to wear it, but take it just in case: warm clothing, boots you can put on in layers, gloves, hat, and sunglasses. Make sure your vehicle is ready too: keep the snow tires on, carry chains, top off the gas tank before you leave town. A stash of food and water doesn't hurt. And don't forget the binoculars.

Given the right conditions, outdoor buffs need venture only nine miles from Butte for an afternoon of backcountry skiing, snowshoeing, hiking, or mountain biking. The trailhead is at the top of Harding Way on Highway 2, along the Continental Divide at elevation 6,453 feet. Park at the Continental Divide Sign. Cross the highway, continuing through a meadow and up a steep road into the trees. At the top is a barbed-wire fence and gate. The trail that leads to the left is a relatively easy one-mile loop that should pose no major challenges to skiers. The trail that leads to the right is a favorite of mountain bikers after the snow melts. It proceeds three or so miles, provid-ing several climbs that will get your heart beating.

The trail ends at what the locals call the Beaver Ponds. Here, you can turn around and retrace your tracks. The more daring proceed down the drainage, though the area is poorly marked. Be sure to take a topographical map should you decide to take this route. Be aware that parts of the trail are narrow, providing only a handle-bar width between tree trunks.

The Beaver Ponds trail provides weekday solitude

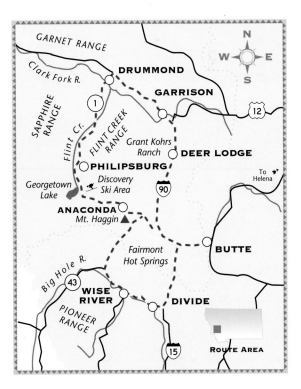

Sunset silhouette
VICTOR H. COLVARD PHOTO

and a wonderful trek through a lodgepole-pine forest. Some areas are open enough to provide vistas of Red Mountain in the Highland Mountains to the south.

BUTTE

Should an outdoor adventure not be to your liking, consider these Butte attractions that are open in early spring:

The Arts Chateau at 321 West Broadway was built for Charles Clark, son of W.A. Clark, one of Butte's famous copper kings. Said to be patterned after a chateau in France and built at the turn of the century, the building is an art gallery and museum. Listed on the National Register of Historic Places, the 26-room edifice boasts intricate stained-glass windows, interiors of wood from around the world, hand-painted wallpaper, and a ballroom.

The Berkeley Pit was formerly an open-pit copper mine. Because pumps that once kept groundwater out of the pit have been turned off, the hole—a mile wide and a mile deep—is slowly filling. (Locals jokingly call it Lake Berkeley.) Check out the viewing stand on Continental Drive for a spectacular look at this awesome sight: colors of the opened earth range from browns and grays to brilliant turquoise and green, and provide an unusual, scenic backdrop to the eerie, poisoned waters of the pit. Looking straight across the pit, you can see where open pit mining continues today.

The World Museum of Mining, west of Montana Tech, opens for the season early in April. You can walk through an 1899 mining camp, learn about the inner workings of an early-day mine, and view thousands of mining-related artifacts. There is an excellent walking tour as well as an interesting collection of rock and mineral specimens.

ANACONDA

Driving west through the city of Anaconda, turn right onto Main Street (the first stop light.) Proceed north on Main across the railroad tracks to Pennsylvania Street and turn left. This paved back road runs by Washoe Park, where you can view trout in the fish hatchery or walk along Warm Springs Creek, which will be swollen with runoff.

Washoe Park is a wonderful place for a picnic. The 100-year-old cottonwood trees may be budding if the weather has been warm. The hatchery, operated by the state of Montana, allows visitors to observe trout at various stages of development. Kids will love this.

Should your visit keep you overnight in Anaconda, be sure to stop by the Washoe Theater. Listed on the National Register of Historic Places, the theater, built in 1936, is a showpiece. Out-of-town visitors are often stunned

The C.W. Clark mansion in Butte
JOHN REDDY PHOTO

by its elegance. The Lussy family keeps the theater running on a shoestring budget, showing films most every night and staging concerts. The Washoe has been beautifully maintained.

Driving west on Cable Road from Washoe Park, look south for one of the most spectacular views of 10,610-foot Mount Haggin in the Anaconda Range. Cable Road rejoins Highway 1, which you can drive toward Georgetown Lake. The vistas of the Anaconda Range continue. About eight miles west of Anaconda, look for the Ana-

conda Job Corps sign on the right side of the road and take a right turn onto Forest Road 195. Drive as far as the snow conditions allow, then ski, hike, or snowshoe on the road, which meanders through a lodgepole pine forest in the spectacular Foster Creek drainage. Views of limestone cliffs high above the canyon floor are breathtaking. Foster Creek riparian areas offer an occasional glimpse of moose and elk.

Upon returning to Montana 1, turn west (or, right) and proceed two more miles. Look for the roadside information sign about the Atlantic Cable mine at the top of Spring Hill. Just past the sign, turn left and proceed about 100 yards down the graveled road. There, beneath another memo-

rable view of the Anaconda Range, you will find a spring-fed fountain with potable water. It's a popular spot with the locals and worth the stop for a drink of cold, fresh water.

GEORGETOWN & DISCOVERY BASIN SKI AREA

Proceeding toward Georgetown Lake, you'll approach Silver Lake on the south side of the highway. The Sapphire Mountains rise in the far distance. The Sapphires divide the Flint Creek and Bitterroot valleys. A few miles farther and Georgetown Lake is seen on the left.

Georgetown is a popular fishery: be extra cautious about going out on any spring ice or you may

end up underneath it. Georgetown contains brookies, rainbows,
and kokanee salmon. Regulations
for fishing Montana's various
streams and lakes vary with the
season, so get up-to-date information before dropping a line in any
of Montana's lakes or streams.

Call to see if Discovery Basin is
still open (406-563-2184). Spring
storms can often dump large
amounts of snow, making March
skiing at Discovery a delight. Even

if you don't hit the slopes, stop
for lunch at the ski lodge where
Dora Goodman, a renowned
Anaconda cook, heads the cafete-
ria crew. The food is remarkable:
homemade soups and breads,
Dora's Italian entrees, and melt-
in-your-mouth chocolate chip
cookies.

Discovery's last parking lot has
a trailhead and map display of
national forest trails, so even if
the downhill ski area is closed you

can cross country ski. Some of
the loops take no more than two
hours to complete. Difficulty
ranges from easy to moderate.
Much of the trail system takes you
through the trees, but some sections climb enough to offer vistas
of the surrounding mountains.
Listen for the noisy Clark's nut-
crackers and watch for elk along
the way. For trail conditions and
information, call the Philipsburg
Ranger District at 859-3211.

Warren Peak in the Pintlers,
from Georgetown Lake
JOHN REDDY PHOTO

NORTH TO PHILIPSBURG

Back on Montana Route 1, drive toward Philipsburg. Flint Creek cuts through a narrow canyon near the pass and several turnouts provide safe areas for drivers to stop and gawk. On the far side of the canyon, high above Flint Creek, you can see the pipeline that once carried water down the canyon and into the Flint Creek Valley, from a dam and generating plant.

The geology here is worth noting. According to *Roadside Geology of the Northern Rockies,* you can observe "huge slabs of red, yellow, and green Precambrian mudstones…[containing] spectacular displays of ripple marks, mudcracks, raindrop imprints, and other sedimentary features—a natural outdoor museum. Watch for the big, flat surfaces sloping down toward the north side of the highway."

Flint Creek through the valley is classic brown-trout habitat. Ask permission before crossing private land, and prepare for a fine time. In addition to browns, 'bows, cutthroats, and brookies, whitefish put up a good fight. Willows and grasses line the stream, and undercut banks are a favorite hangout for many a scaly inhabitant.

Several abandoned mining camps, such as Granite, surround the old, scenic mining town of Philipsburg, but the spring snowpack may prevent easy access. As an alternative, check out the architecture of "P-burg's" old buildings and houses. Stop by Neal's Photo on the main street and visit with the proprietor, Steve Neal, who is something of a walking history book for the area and is an accomplished photographer. His nondescript shop is an interesting compilation of photo equipment, supplies, and displays.

Twenty miles north of Philipsburg on Montana 1, about 2½ miles south of Hall, turn east on an unmarked gravel road, continue through an assortment of buildings, and proceed for about a mile. Again, you will observe an accumulation of old homes and farm buildings. Welcome to New Chicago.

VIEWS OF LIMESTONE CLIFFS HIGH ABOVE FOSTER CREEK'S CANYON ARE BREATHTAKING

According to Roberta Carkeek Cheney's *Names on the Face of Montana,* New Chicago was named by William Dingwall, "an old-timer who hoped the town would someday equal Chicago, Ill. New Chicago was once a bustling settlement and trade center. Postmaster John Featherman opened a mercantile business there on the old Mullan Trail." The cemetery is several hundred yards from the town. It sits on a bluff and offers a 360-degree vista of the area, including the Flint Creek and Garnet mountain ranges.

DUNKLEBERG PASS

If road conditions permit (it is gumbo in places, which spells trouble in the spring), road trippers can take the Dunkleberg Pass road south from New Chicago, for 12 meandering miles. (Don't even try it without a Deerlodge National Forest visitor/travel map in hand for this adventure.) The road eventually turns north, crosses the old Northern Pacific Railroad tracks (now Montana Rail Link) over a wooden overpass, and deposits travelers at the Jens interchange on Interstate 90, about six miles east of Drummond. The Dunkleberg road proceeds through private property in several areas, so drivers are admonished to stay on the roadway.

The Dunkleberg road is rarely used (which could make it more of an adventure than you might like). It meanders and dips in and out of ravines and skirts benches.

You'll get relatively close-up views of the Flint Creek Range, and a perspective of the countryside not seen from Interstate 90 or Highway 10A. With sagebrush and grasslands comprising the immediate, lowlands scenery, the Dunkleberg road is beautiful because of its remoteness. Don't be surprised to see a coyote race across the road or meadow. Look for other wildlife such as moose, elk, and deer.

DEER LODGE

At Interstate 90, proceed east toward Deer Lodge. There, travelers should consider taking the 38-mile Deer Lodge Circle Tour. Unless there is ice or significant snow, the road is passable for

The Highland Mountains, south of Butte, rise just above 10,000 feet.
RICK & SUSIE GRAETZ PHOTO

automobiles. The trip will give you vistas of the Deer Lodge Valley and surrounding mountains. For a detailed brochure that provides information about grasslands and forests of the area, as well as loop directions, visit the Deer Lodge Chamber of Commerce (846-2094) or the Forest Service (846-1770).

The Clark Fork River through Deer Lodge Valley is a confusion of possibilities for anglers. Its waters are part of the largest Superfund cleanup site in the nation. And yet restoration efforts have produced water that can carry trout.

This section of the Clark Fork has been fought over by irrigators, anglers, miners, loggers, wildlife advocates, fisheries biologists, ranchers, and just about anyone else who ever inhabited or visited the valley. On the plus side of all the haggling and bargaining, polluting and cleaning up, it

would appear that no one is indifferent to the Clark Fork, and that may be its saving grace.

The Montana State Hospital at Warm Springs campus is located near the interstate exit, and offers an array of turn-of-the-century architecture (some of the buildings are slated for demolition). You can drive or walk through the campus. On the west end of the facility is a hot springs spewing from an odd two-story-high cone, and crowned with a cupola.

SOAK, SKI, FISH

Continue east on Interstate 90 and exit at the Opportunity/ Anaconda exit. Take time for a refreshing and relaxing swim in the pools at Fairmont Hot Springs. It is a full-service resort with large swimming pools, a water slide, and plenty of other amenities to entice you and the kids to stay for the weekend—there's nothing

DON'T BE SURPRISED TO SEE A COYOTE RACE ACROSS THE REMOTE DUNKLEBERG ROAD

A spring day's spectacular finale
RICK & SUSIE GRAETZ PHOTO

quite like floating in hot water under the stars.

Back on Route 1 going northwest, turn south at the sign for Wisdom. Highway 274 is paved, but beware of potholes. The highway proceeds seven miles to the top of the Mill Creek Pass, 6,772 feet elevation, and offers spectacular views of the Anaconda Range, including 10,641-foot Mount Evans, and 10,227-foot Short Peak. Motorists should be aware that this remote area is noted for high winds and drifting snow.

Proceed down the pass south several miles to the Mount Haggin Nordic Ski Area. It's managed by volunteers and provides a variety of groomed and ungroomed loops. Some take thirty minutes; others take half a day. It's a nice gesture to drop a few bucks in the donation box at the trailhead. There are no services here, so be sure to bring food and water.

Returning to Highway 274, proceed about 12 miles to the junction of Highway 43, and turn east. Motorists will parallel the scenic and fishing-famous Big Hole River, which may be somewhat free of ice. The river terrain varies from grassy meadows with wide meanders to picture-perfect mountain stream with boulders, riffles, and deep pools.

The town of Wise River is located 11 miles from the Highway 274 junction, at the convergence of the Wise River and the Big Hole River. (Hamburgers at the Wise River restaurant-bar will satisfy even the heartiest of appetites). This section of highway, although narrow with no shoulder, offers excellent bicycling. Although the 90-mile Butte-Mill Creek-Wise River-Divide-Butte loop is a favorite of local road cyclists, many shorter segments are equally as enjoyable, particularly the 23-mile stretch from the Highway 43-274 junction through the canyon to Divide, 12 miles east of Wise River.

The road connecting Wise River to Polaris is a designated National Forest Scenic Byway. Portions are closed by snow each winter, so check on conditions before embarking on that route as a side trip.

HOME AGAIN

From Divide, travelers can proceed east two miles to Interstate 15, and travel north back to Butte. The route offers scenic views of 9,436-foot Mount Fleecer to the west, and the Humbug Spires in the Highlands, to the east. Fleecer is a popular elk range—use binoculars to find them in the meadows.

Whether you opt to explore the entire route in one day, or take it in portions, one thing is certain: You will observe some of Montana's most spectacular scenery, from snowcapped peaks and golden sandstone cliffs to lakes and blue-ribbon trout streams and rivers. It's a trip sure to leave you with a better understanding and appreciation of why this is called Big Sky Country. ✧

Water, Wind, & Wheat

by Elizabeth and Wilbur Wood

DRIVE INTO THE SEMI-ARID HINTERLANDS OF NORTHEASTERN MONTANA AND YOU'LL LIKELY BE ATTRACTED to water. Lewistown, with the third-largest freshwater spring in the world, is a place to satisfy that urge. Big Spring produces ninety million gallons of pure, sweet, wonderful water a day.

People come to Lewistown for events such as the Trappers Association Meeting, the Fiddlers Convention, and the Fair, or with plans to visit ghost towns and an old mining camp, or to fish and hike in the surrounding mountains. Lewistown is an appealing and hospitable getaway.

The largest city between Great Falls and Billings, Lewistown is the geographic center of the state. The economy has traditionally depended on cattle and wheat, and intermittent gold mining, but outdoor recreation is fast becoming part of the town's character. Other small industries include the water from Big Spring that is sold all over the state, and the best cat litter on the planet, made by Mountain Meadow Cat Litter (we tell you this from experience).

Drive down Main Street in morning sunlight, past the gleaming dome of the Fergus County Courthouse built in 1907, and note the attractiveness of this active community. While most of the east half of Montana has been losing population over the last

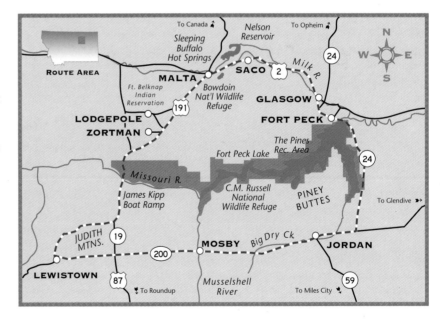

Woodhawk Bottom, Missouri River breaks west of Highway 191
KENT & CHARLENE KRONE PHOTO

decade, Lewistown has held its own, and still is a full-service town. You can get your computer repaired, find replacement parts for your tractor, buy fancy hiking boots or solid work boots from friendly and helpful people. 618 Main serves an excellent cup of coffee, regular or espresso, and the scrumptious bagels made locally by Johnson's Bakery. Also in that building is The Yoga Center, as well as an excellent sporting goods store with helpful personnel.

Big Spring park and trout hatchery
GAIL JACKSON PHOTO

Downtown's well-preserved brick and stone buildings add charm and grace: Nearly twenty sites within the city limits are on the National Register of Historic Places and they are featured on a self-guided walking tour. Museums, forts, trading posts, and old mining camps, in the city or the surrounding hills, beckon history buffs or those with active children.

The graceful Carnegie Library, built in 1906, has computer links to national resources, and extras such as course information for Montana State University classes in Lewistown, and information on Habitat for Humanity.

Lewistown is part small town and part tourist town. Residents told us about an unadvertised bed and breakfast in a historic mansion downtown. There are several better-known bed and breakfasts at nearby ranches. You can also stay at motels or the Yogo Inn.

The Lewistown Art Museum shows paintings and sculpture from its permanent collection, as well as displaying temporary exhibits. The gift shop sells only Montana-made items, including a good selection of prints, sculpture, jewelry, pottery, and weaving. There are other galleries in town with paintings and prints at reasonable prices. For those seeking Western art, look into the Moccasin Mountain gallery for your prize.

If you want a traditional Montana drinking spot with a good dance floor, you can sip a brew at the Montana Tavern on Main Street. A bonus there includes their viewing box: peer down to see Big Spring Creek flowing underground beneath downtown Lewistown. Patrons have seen beavers, muskrats, and ducks paddling downstream, and a few have dropped in a line and caught rainbow trout!

If you want to select your drink from dozens of imported or micro-brewery beers, step next door to The Whole Famdamily for a truly great bowl of homemade soup, and a sandwich. Do try their specialty desserts. This is friendly family atmosphere at its best. We also like the chili at the Poor Man's Books and Coffee, where you can browse used books before eating your fill.

As the self-proclaimed "official chocolate-ice-cream-soda-tasters of eastern Montana," we can recommend the art deco soda fountain at the Bon Ton Sweet Shop.

During the summer months, don't miss an outing on the Charlie Russell Chew-Choo, which provides dinner and entertainment before returning at twilight. The train crosses several trestles and goes through a tunnel on its route through the open spaces of central Montana. You're likely to see wildlife such as mule deer and pronghorn antelope.

For further details about Lewistown's activities, contact the Chamber of Commerce, Box 818, Lewistown, MT 59457 or call (800) 216-5436.

OUT AND ABOUT

Central Montana is a jewel. The region sports backcountry campgrounds, lakes, and mountainous areas for hiking and fishing. Trout-stocked Crystal Lake is a popular weekend destination in the Big Snowies. Others water-ski on Ackley Lake, a prairie reservoir forty-five minutes west of town. Or try a little fishing and a picnic, followed by a dip in Warm Springs, thirty minutes north of town. The State Fish Hatchery, about five miles south of Lewistown, has a picnic area and interpretive displays, and Hanson Creek Recreation Area (good fishing) is a few miles upstream.

Hiking maps are available from Lewis and Clark National Forest, Judith Ranger District, Stanford, MT 59479, and maps of the Missouri Breaks badlands country are available from Bureau of Land Management, Lewistown District, Box 1160, Lewistown, MT 59457. For information on hiking and auto tours, campsites, and other recreation along the Missouri from Sand Creek to Fort Peck Dam, in the Charles M. Russell National Wildlife Refuge, contact the CMR, Box 110, Lewistown, MT 59457.

THE MIGHTY MO

If water attracted you to the cradle of mountains surrounding Lewistown, water—along with wildlife and dinosaur bones—may lure you out of that cradle, northeast into the remote high plains, toward the Missouri River and Fort Peck Reservoir.

As you drive north on Highway 191, the Judith Mountains adorn the view from your passenger window. Six miles beyond the tiny town of Roy, top off your gas tank and try a bowl of homemade soup at Bohemian Corners Cafe. North again, and the Little Rocky Mountains jump into view, a blue ship floating on a rumpled prairie sea—they are the main visible landform

The Charlie Russell Chew-Choo
JIM JACKSON PHOTO

dominating this journey.

The other dominant landform is the Missouri River, but here the river is mostly invisible until you're nearly on top of it. Forced south of its pre-Ice Age riverbed by the continental ice sheet, the river has carved a geologically recent channel through some two hundred miles of north-central Montana, so the country along the river is rugged, creased by deep forested canyons. It's home to elk, deer, and bighorn sheep, as well as summer-grazing cattle, horses, and domestic sheep. Rafters and canoeists float this stretch of the Missouri, and the C.M. Russell National Wildlife Refuge offers hiking, camping, boating, fishing, and—in season—hunting. Beware, however, of trusting even a four-wheel-drive vehicle off the highway: rain

turns unpaved roads here to a sticky "gumbo" and as the CMR's pamphlets and signs warn: "Back country travel is impossible when roads are wet." You should believe every word of that warning.

The James Kipp Recreation Area is a great place for a picnic under the cottonwoods and a swim in the Missouri. We like to stake our tent here for two or three days, slide our canoe into the river, check out the herons and beavers, and hike trails in some of the wildest country in Montana.

LITTLE ROCKIES

Continuing north across the Fred Robinson Bridge, you climb until again the Little Rockies fill your windshield. If you haven't spotted it sooner, you can't miss the long pale gash between dark forested peaks. This is the recently de-

activated Zortman-Landusky Mine, which was the largest open-pit, cyanide-heap-leach gold and silver operation in Montana, owned by a Canadian-based corporation, Pegasus Gold.

The Gros Ventre and Assiniboine tribes of the Fort Belknap Reservation, bordering the mine to the north, persistently voiced concerns about the mine's effect on both water quantity and water quality. The mine pumped enormous amounts of water for ore processing. Cyanide-treated ore releases heavy metals and other contaminants which must be contained. A short side trip will get you a closer look at the reclamation operations. Turn north onto Highway 66, climb up and over a shoulder of the Little Rockies, then turn into the reservation town of Hays. The road curves south along a creek into Mission Canyon, past the powwow grounds, to a fork. Drive left and you'll switchback up a slope to a locked gate and a very limited view of the mine. Or go right,

park along the road, stay on the reservation side of the fence, and climb a few thousand feet up flat-topped Mission Peak for an eagle's-eye view of the massive pit, roads, and ponds—from which you can lift your eyes for long views of prairies and mountains.

From Hays you can parallel the forested north slope of the "Island Mountains" (as the Assiniboine call them) to Lodgepole, then southeast back to Highway 191. You can also dip into the mining town of Zortman, where the bar had decent choices of country songs on its jukebox the last time we stopped in.

MALTA'S BONES

Highway 191 ends—or begins—in Malta. Uncertainty about the mine's future has forced recent layoffs, but mine reclamation workers still commute the nearly fifty miles from Malta to the Little Rockies. Pegasus, while it was the largest taxpayer in the county, clearly propped up the local economy: clean streets, neat homes,

Fort Peck Reservoir
CHARLIE BORLAND/DEFINITIVE STOCK PHOTO

no empty storefronts. But since no mine can last forever, what comes next?

Nate Murphy has one answer: dinosaur bones. They poke out of hillsides and eroding streambeds from Saco to Jordan and beyond. Murphy has unearthed many himself—including a *Tyrannosaurus rex* and an extremely well preserved crested duckbill, or Hadrosaur, ancient giants that flourished here some seventy-five million years ago when this was lush flat country with meandering streams flowing into a narrow sea. Murphy sees dino bones as a non-renewable resource, like gold, and he wants more of them to stay in this country, studied in place and housed in on-site museums, rather than see them hauled off to museums far away.

For Murphy, who explores,

conducts digs and workshops, and prepares fossils for universities and museums, this has meant months and years of volunteer work helping the local historical society raise over $200,000 to relocate the Phillips County Museum to spacious quarters in a former sporting goods store on Highway 2. The museum plans to feature displays on native cultures, cattle drives, homesteaders, and the last big train holdup (by Kid Curry in Malta in the early 1900s). "But the dinosaur display will be our hook," Murphy emphasized, noting the casts of a T-rex skull and an *Albertosaurus* skeleton, along with the Hadrosaur he discovered.

For more information on the museum, as well as details on how to participate in exciting digs such as the one near Saco that unearthed a group of Hadrosaurs that were probably drowned and then later gnawed upon by T-rexes, contact Nate Murphy at Box 429, Malta, MT 59538, or phone (406) 654-2323.

THE HI-LINE
East along Highway 2 from Malta to Glasgow, we recommend: Bowdoin National Wildlife Refuge, especially for birdwatching; Nelson Reservoir for boating and fishing; and Sleeping Buffalo Hot Springs' cabins, gift shop,

DINOSAUR BONES POKE OUT OF HILLSIDES AND ERODING STREAMBEDS FROM SACO TO JORDAN AND BEYOND

cafe, steakhouse, hot and hotter indoor pools, and a high slide into an outdoor pool. Saco offers a bed and breakfast, bar, cafe, motel, and antiques store. At Hinsdale, Highway 2 crosses the Milk River—this is the ancient valley of the Missouri.

You can take a little side trip that gets you closer to the river by turning off onto a cottonwood-lined secondary road that leads through Vandalia and Tampico into Glasgow.

GLASGOW AND FORT PECK
Glasgow's stone and brick downtown buildings remind us of Lewistown's charm, and this is also a "full-service" town. Plenty of motels, a choice of good restaurants, the Pioneer Museum, and a store that reminds us what it's like to try to make a living in eastern Montana: You get by doing a little of this and a little of that. In this case, one store houses video rentals, a tanning salon, and a coffee shop with espresso and cappuccino. Quite a mix.

It's twenty miles down Highway 24 to Fort Peck Dam, a gigantic Corps of Engineers' power and irrigation project built during the Depression, 1933 to 1937. It backs up the Missouri River into a reservoir 134 miles long, with a 1,600-mile shoreline. You can select from boating, fishing, water sports, a museum, and tours of the dam. In the former government town of Fort Peck, a lively and thriving summer theater provides excellent family entertainment. Call the Fort Peck Fine Arts Council, 228-9219, or Jim Smrcka at 228-9391 for exact dates and ticket info.

South of Fort Peck, a series of basins are punctuated by fantastic eroding landforms. You'll keep wondering if you're at the top yet, but Highway 24 keeps dipping and rising until at last it levels off

and then descends to the junction with Highway 200, and the 166-mile run west to Lewistown.

THE BIG DRY
Sagebrush, junipers, dry gulches, knobby ridgetops—this is tough country to wring out a living, but people hanging on here soften this toughness with humor. End of the World—12 Miles. Jordan, Montana—15 Miles reads the caption on a foam cup-holder in a dry goods store in Jordan, where the Garfield County Museum shares space with the Senior Citizen Center; shops and stores in the three-block business section provide basic services, and the Jordan Drugstore serves a chocolate ice cream soda meeting all specifications. Beneath the deer and antelope heads in the Hell Creek Bar, consuming a burger and fries with a beer, you may pick up a lesson in local economics when a man complains about problems with his new pickup, and the bartender chides: "Nobody forced you to buy that pickup in Billings. You could've got one in Miles City, or Circle...."

Mountains sprout beyond your windshield and pines dot the land near Mosby, on the Musselshell River. Southeast of Winnett, Petrolia Reservoir offers fishing, boating, and camping.

Fifteen miles west of Grass Range (good country cooking in the cafe), you can take another side trip. Turn north onto a gravel road for a stunning drive through the Judith Mountains. You'll pass the vivid blue house at Abbott Guest Ranch, the old mining town of Giltedge, and then climb up a narrow canyon to a high ridge and up Judith Peak with its great panoramic views. The route then descends and passes another mining town, Maiden. From there, a paved road takes you back to Highway 191 and the trip south to Lewistown. ✧

SUMMER

Vast, Vigorous, & Varied

by Dorothy Rustebakke

SWEEPING VISTAS OF PRAIRIE GRASSLANDS, STRIP-PATTERNED WHEAT FIELDS, TIME-ETCHED BADLANDS, SCENIC river valleys, and the biggest, bluest sky you've ever seen—that's Montana's northeast corner. You'll also find rodeos, powwows, intriguing places to shop, museums, art galleries, and friendly small towns along this 240-mile loop.

GLENDIVE AND MAKOSHIKA

Glendive, located along the Yellowstone River on Interstate 94, is a great place to start your northeast Montana weekender. The city's many attractions include re-created pioneer-era buildings at the Frontier Gateway Museum, an art gallery, a downtown walking tour, a variety of shops, agate hunting along the Yellowstone River, and nearby Makoshika State Park.

"Totally awesome!" exclaimed my grandson when we entered Makoshika. I agreed. We were surrounded by odd-shaped pinnacles, hogback ridges, fantasy-shaped hoodoos, and barren moonscape buttes fringed by green patches of ponderosa pines, junipers, sagebrush, cactus, and range grass. From the higher elevations we had a spectacular view of this strange, rugged land created by centuries of erosion.

Coyotes, mule deer, bobcats, eagles, and turkey vultures inhabit this picturesque 8,123-acre state park, but they seem pretty tame compared to the prehistoric animals that once roamed here. Take a look at the triceratops skull and other fossils on display at the visitor center!

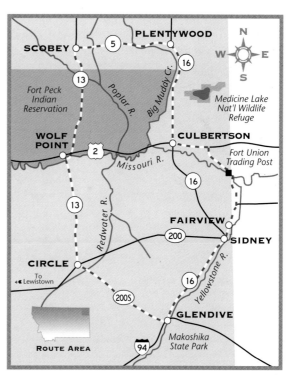

Films and exhibits at the visitor center take you back to the time when eastern Montana was a subtropical coastal plain. Maps available at the center show established trails, interpretive sites, campgrounds, and picnic areas. Stick to the paved all-weather roads if the weather is wet or if heights make you nervous.

Memorial Day through Labor Day the park is open from 10 a.m. to 6 p.m. seven days a week. Winter hours are 9 a.m. to 5 p.m. weekdays, and 1 to 5 p.m. Sun-

FACING PAGE: *Fort Union, 1800s trading post on the Missouri River*
LARRY MAYER PHOTO

PRECEDING PAGE: *Hoodoos and spires in Makoshika State Park*
LARRY MAYER PHOTO

days. Call 365-6256 for additional information. Sunday morning church services are held in the amphitheater throughout the summer.

In downtown Glendive, enjoy some fine Italian food at Bacios Italian Ristorante, or a hearty sandwich and a brew at the Beer Jug, which also supplies fishing information and tackle.

The Hostetler House Bed and Breakfast is a delightful place to spend the night. It's a charming 1912 home with country decor and a breakfast menu featuring homemade breads and muffins (phone 365-4505). The Best Western Jordan Motor Inn is a full-service hotel (phone 800-824-5067). Even if you don't stay at the Jordan you're welcome to view the impressive Ed Klapmeier agate collection in the lobby, and the J.K. Ralston paintings.

Glendive was established by the Northern Pacific in 1881 as a railroad town, and for almost ninety years it was a division headquarters. The railroad continues to be important to the city's economy, and their modernized shop services Burlington Northern Santa Fe trains. Agriculture, however, plays the most important part in the area's economy, and oil is also a factor. Glendive benefits, too, from having Dawson Community College located there.

Agate hunting along the Yellowstone River is an enjoyable family activity, as are guided raft trips. Check with the chamber of commerce for information.

If your trip is between May 16 and June 30 you might want to try snagging one of those seventy- or eighty-pound paddlefish at the Intake diversion dam fifteen miles north of Glendive. Two-day fishing permits and paddlefish tags are available for out-of-staters, and fishing gear can be rented at the site. Your fish will be cleaned, cut, wrapped, and frozen for you in exchange for the eggs, which are used to make caviar.

SIDNEY

Adjoining the Yellowstone River north toward Sidney are numerous irrigated fields full of sugar beets, alfalfa, beans, corn, and potatoes. In the higher country are fields of hard spring wheat and other small grains. Working oil pumps scattered along the route are a reminder that the entire area is part of the Williston Basin. The oil industry has had a "boom and bust" effect on many area towns.

Harmon's Agate and Silver shop at Crane is known for its beautiful display of Montana agates and for the craftsmanship of its owners. You can have your own agates custom-crafted there into fine jewelry, or buy stones already set in a three-color Black Hills gold-silver overlay.

Sidney is in the heart of sugar-beet country, and the large Holly Sugar refinery is a major employer in this town of 5,200. The Mon-Dak Heritage Center houses an art gallery and a well-furnished pioneer town. Other art treasures may be found at the Cabin Creek and Bear Paw galleries, and in several shops that consign the arts and crafts made by locals.

For a soul-satisfying steak dinner try The South 40 or the Triangle Nite Club. Both have received the Montana Cowbelles' "Montana Beefbacker" award.

FAIRVIEW

Fairview claims to be the Sugar Beet Capital of Montana and North Dakota, since the town straddles the border between both states. It also straddles two different time zones. It is a friendly little town, with a nice park for swimming, picnicking, or relaxing.

The Fairview bridge that once carried railroad and automobile traffic across the Yellowstone River three miles east of town is the only lift bridge on the Yellowstone River and has been designated a National Historic Site. The Snowden Bridge, another lift bridge ten miles north of Fairview on the Missouri River, is still used by the railroad. Both bridges are worth a visit.

Ten miles north of Fairview is the reconstructed Fort Union Trading Post, one of those "don't miss" attractions, especially if you have children or history buffs in your group. This post dominated the Upper Missouri River fur trade between 1829 and 1867. During

Yellowstone River
LARRY MAYER PHOTO

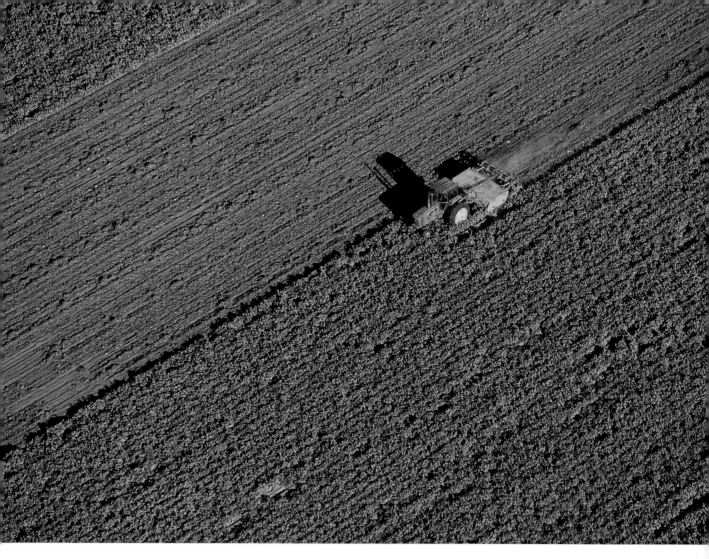

Sugar beet harvest near Sidney
LARRY MAYER PHOTO

the annual Fort Union Fur Traders Rendezvous participants dress and camp like 19th-century fur traders. The fort has other "living history" demonstrations throughout the summer.

For a hospitable touch of country elegance in a beautiful log cabin, stay overnight at the Montana River Ranch, nestled in a grove of cottonwood trees on the Missouri River nine miles northwest of Fort Union. I enjoy the antique furnishings, rustic surroundings, and home-cooked breakfasts (other meals and picnic lunches available by request). It's a peaceful place to relax or to take a nature walk before or after a day of travel. For reservations, call 769-2127.

ON TO CULBERTSON

Culbertson was established in 1887 as a railroad shipping point for livestock. It was a rip-roaring cowtown, and at one time thirteen saloons—open twenty-four hours a day—lined the three-block main street.

The town's past is faithfully preserved in its museum and celebrations. The Lakota Connection in the east end of the Coach Bar on Highway 2 has everything from Indian-made quilts to diamond willow canes on display and for sale.

MEDICINE LAKE AND PLENTYWOOD

A visit to the Medicine Lake National Wildlife Refuge is like a step back in time. The beauty and serenity of the prairie is as it used to be before plows destroyed the native grasses. The eight-mile-long

lake and its surrounding terrain attract as many as 75,000 birds at times. You can get an unobstructed view of the area from a hundred-foot-high observation tower at the visitor center. ("Awesome" once again!) A fourteen-mile self-guided auto tour takes you to the tipi hills, where rings of stone mark century-old Indian campsites, and the gull islands, where thousands of pelicans, blue herons, double-crested cormorants, and Canada geese build their nests. A pair of powerful binoculars mounted on the newly constructed Bridgerman Point observation platform offers a close-up view of the largest colonies of white pelicans in the United States.

Next stop is Plentywood, named by outlaw Dutch Henry, who found "plenty wood" there for his gang's campfires. This attractive town, population 2,100,

has parks, a swimming pool, and an interesting history presented at the Sheridan County Museum. Old-timers can tell some fascinating tales about the Depression years when Charles Taylor used the Plentywood *Producer News* to promote Soviet-style communism in Montana.

The Civic Center, near the museum, houses a seventy-four-foot-long mural painted by Whitetail artist Bob Southland, depicting the history of Sheridan County from the days of Indians and fur traders to the present.

Randy's Restaurant on the west edge of town is where many of the locals gather for good everyday dining. For soup and sandwiches, try Laura Belle's on Main Street. It's also the place to view or purchase wall decorations featuring wildlife and rural scenes crafted from native woods by Bill and Margaret Wagner, a rural

Plentywood couple whose work was chosen for display in Japan in a 1992 cultural exchange. You will find hand-woven baskets there, too.

The Hilltop House Bed and Breakfast at Westby (phone 385-2533), twenty-six miles east of Plentywood, is a unique place to spend the night. From the upstairs windows you can watch the sun set across Montana, then come up the next morning from North Dakota. You can see north across the border into Canada. They also sell antiques and gifts.

SCOBEY

I'm especially proud of Scobey, my own hometown. It's a lively community of 1,200 people, and is probably the only town of its size in the country with a full-fledged symphony orchestra. It's also a sports-minded town, and the old-timers recall when former

Medicine Lake National Wildlife Refuge
LARRY MAYER PHOTO

Chicago White Sox players "Swede" Risberg and "Happy" Felsch, who were ousted from major league baseball for "throwing" a World Series game, were recruited for a Scobey team that steam-rolled over its rivals during the 1920s. The 1996-97 girls' and boys' high school athletic teams won their share of championships, too.

The area's past is recalled in Daniels County Pioneer Town. Forty-two homestead-era buildings, restored and furnished, are open to visitors between Memorial Day and Labor Day, and by appointment at other times. The renovated theater there is the site of the rollicking Dirty Shame home-talent shows during Pioneer Days. A downtown art show that same weekend features the work of area artists. Other summer events include the Lions Club's "Big Roar" that features a well-known country music entertainer, an old-fashioned Fourth of July celebration topped off with the Jimmy Dean Country Showdown talent show and fireworks, and the Daniels County Fair.

Scobey's economy depends mostly on hard red spring wheat and other small grains. The Nemont Telephone Cooperative headquarters is also a major employer.

Tasty oriental cuisine is available at Shu's Kitchen at the east edge of Scobey. Steaks and seafood are specialties at the Slipper Lounge Restaurant and Casino in Scobey and at Whiskey Buttes, nine miles west of town. For reservations at Scobey's largest motel, the Cattle King, call 487-5332.

American white pelican at Medicine Lake NWR shading its youngster from the sun
PHOTO COURTESY U.S. FISH & WILDLIFE SERVICE

The Outlaw Caves, where the early-day rustlers holed up after they skipped across the border, are near Coronach, Saskatchewan, twenty-five miles northwest of Scobey. The five-hour-long Big Muddy tour to the caves is quite fascinating. For reservations phone 306-267-3312.

WOLF POINT

Wolf Point, on the Fort Peck Indian Reservation, still has much of the ambiance of bygone days. Step into the unpretentious saddlery on Main Street and browse among the saddles and boots and other Western gear. They still make saddles there, as well as custom-tooled belts and billfolds. You'll find just the right outfit to wear to the Wolf Point Wild Horse Stampede in mid-July. It's one of the biggest and best rodeos in the state, and is also the oldest.

The Sherman Motor Inn offers fine dining and is also a comfortable place to spend the night (800-952-1100). For country and antique decor and a taste of ranch life in the Missouri River valley, choose the Forsness Farm Bed and Breakfast west of Wolf Point. You can join the family in ranch chores, take a stroll along paths where whitetail deer, bald eagles, great-horned owls and numerous other birds and animals may be seen, or just relax after a hearty breakfast that includes homemade breads and muffins. Call 653-2492 for reservations.

Interested in antique tractors? Visit Louis Toavs at his farm ten miles north of Wolf Point. He has collected more than 500 John Deere tractors, one of every model made from 1923 to 1953. Call him at 392-5224 to make sure he's home and get the directions to his place.

FULL CIRCLE

As you drive south from Wolf Point on Highway 13 you will

DANIELS COUNTY PIONEER TOWN OFFERS FORTY-TWO HOMESTEAD-ERA BUILDINGS, EACH RESTORED AND FURNISHED

cross the Missouri on a new concrete bridge. Nearby stands the higher steel Lewis and Clark Bridge built in 1930 to handle Model T's. That picturesque old five-span bridge is listed on the National Register of Historic Places, and is being preserved by the Montana Historical Society.

Circle got its name from the circle brand of a big cattle company that during the late 1800s drove its longhorns from Texas to the fine grasslands here along the Redwater River. You can take a dip in the town's public swimming pool or relax in the park while the kids work off some of their energy in the well-equipped playground east of Main Street. At the southwest edge of town is the McCone County Museum, where history and taxidermy combine to make interesting exhibits. For Western art, stop in at the Candlelight Gallery, where local artist Candy Witte displays her wildlife paintings on sandstone, bone, plates, and canvas.

From Circle it's forty-nine miles past vast fields of grain and hilly pastureland back to Glendive. Lots of wide-open spaces and big sky fill your eyes and your memories as you leave Montana's northeastern prairie country and say "goodby" to the friendly, hardy folks who live here. ✧

Frontier, Floats, & Footpaths

by Beverly R. Magley

I CALL IT A "SURF AND TURF" WEEKEND. YOU KNOW: A DAY ON THE RIVER AND A DAY IN THE MOUNTAINS. THIS 140-mile weekend route circling the Tobacco Roots covers Montana's premier surf and turf territory. First, there are those unbeatable blue-ribbon fishing rivers. Then there are numerous routes into the Tobacco Roots.

Ever been accused of wanting it all? No problem. This is the place.

There's just one hitch. This Weekender starts in Virginia City and it's remarkably easy to spend the entire weekend there. The boardwalk has a pleasing creak when you walk along the main street. The dry, grassy hills around town are a muted gold. A person could sit a while on the shady veranda of the Fairweather Inn and people-watch. It's an 1800s kind of thing to do.

HISTORY ALIVE

Virginia City is not just another fakey Old West tourist trap. There are some regular touristy things to do, but authenticity here makes it unique. The McGovern sisters' dry goods store, for example, looks exactly the way it did when the sisters walked out in 1939 and never returned. I opened the top box on one shelf and found it half full of spools of thread, in shades

The Tobacco Roots, from Ramshorn Peak
GEORGE WUERTHNER PHOTO

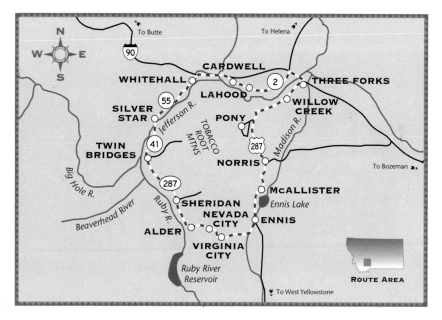

of pink. The box below was three quarters full, in reds. Below, another box was chock full of reds.

This is the real thing. Sure, you can dress up in period clothes and get an "old-tyme photo" taken, or attend the theater and be thoroughly entertained by turn of the century humor, but take a close look at your playbill. It was hand-

set with old lead or wood type, printed by hand on the 1860s Washington Press in the *Montana Post* offices a few doors up the street. The *Post* was Montana's first newspaper.

It's a marvel to watch John Ellingsen make those playbills. First, there are dozens of fonts, or type styles, and he has to figure out which ones have enough of the right letters left to print that particular offering. Then there are the "cuts," those engraved patterns and curlicues of that time. He places each letter and cut in a form, fitting the whole within a thousandth of an inch. Then he carries the form to the press, turns the crank and slides it in on silent bearings more than a hundred years old.

John loves this place. He has been curator in Virginia City/Nevada City for twenty-five years and his knowledge is astounding. "Charlie Bovey wanted the public to come and see this collection and enjoy it," he said. "He tried to make things look like they would have been—clocks on the walls, a gold scale,

Virginia City's main street
SCOTT WHEELER PHOTO

a shelf of glasses. Things the way they really were, not presented like a case full of museum items that don't relate to each other."

We poked around the old jewelry store, where artisans once made adornments from a miner's own gold. The old Virginia City telephone switchboard was stored in the back room. It was taken out of service in 1958, and at my prompting John peered closer at the attached names. "Well, look at that," he murmured. "Some of them still live here."

Virginia and Nevada City residents may cater to the past, but they also have their share of present-day realities. Charles A. and Sue Ford Bovey have passed away, and the buildings and collections they owned need major attention and money. The state of Montana purchased the buildings

and contents, thus saving the treasures from the auction block. Residents need to revise their zoning plan, build a new water tank, figure out how to keep the town vital without sacrificing historic attractions. They're up to the task, though, and community spirit remains high. Mayor Bob Gabler talked with pride of their volunteerism (for example, each spring he rounds up people with shovels to go clear the culverts of ice), and their homemade entertainment, from a spontaneous "Dog-in-a-Wheelbarrow Race" one summer to an annual top-hats-and-ball-gowns Victorian Ball.

I like to stay in the creaky Fairweather Inn (800-648-7588) or one of the bed and breakfast establishments. Pat Vanderbeck hosts travelers in the Wilbur Fisk Sanders Guest Home (843-5473).

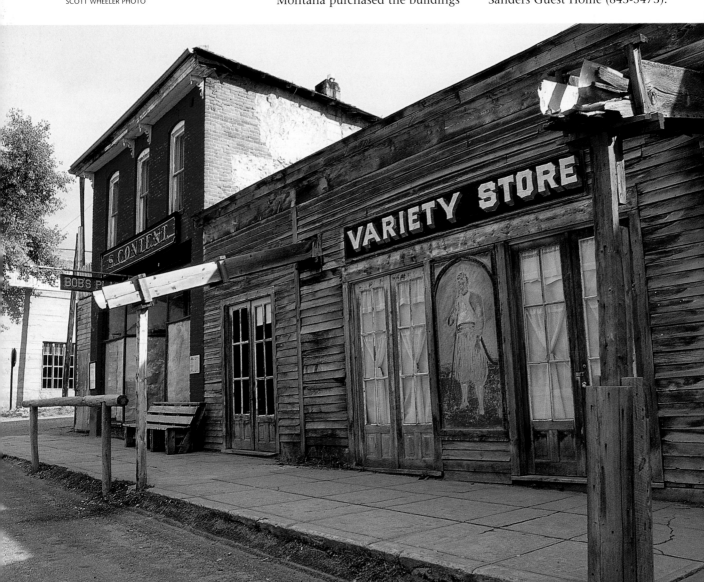

THE PLEASANT TOWN OF TWIN BRIDGES IS KNOWN FOR FISHING: RODS, GUIDES, LODGES

Sanders was an attorney who successfully prosecuted the infamous road agents in 1863, in the middle of the Vigilante era. Sanders was later elected to the U.S. Senate. More recently, another prominent prosecuting attorney spent time in Virginia City. In 1985, Marc Racicot successfully tried renegade mountain men Dan and Don Nichols in Virginia City. Racicot was later elected governor of Montana. Could there be a pattern here?

Carma and John Sinerius have hauled in two old cabins and converted them to comfortable lodgings at Just An Experience Bed & Breakfast (843-5402) right next to Nevada City. Besides the pleasant surroundings, I'd go back again for another round of whole wheat-sunflower-barley pancakes with chokecherry syrup.

ALONG THE RUBY
Just south of Alder, Ruby River Reservoir provides liquid relief from the heat. Swim, picnic, camp, fish, or just sit on the banks and sift for garnets, then drive to Chick's Bar in Alder for other kinds of liquid relief. Or grab a mighty fine steak at the Alder Steakhouse. Eleven miles north, in Sheridan, Mill Creek Inn serves a fine north-of-the-border Wet Burrito. The menu announces, "If your order doesn't arrive in five minutes, you'll be

served in eight or nine, maybe twelve. Just relax." So order, and while away the minutes playing pool, darts, or shove penny.

Sheridan locals were in an uproar this past spring. Their century-old traditional access to the Ruby River had been closed by new landowners, and nobody was happy about the situation, except maybe the newcomers who now have their own personal piece of paradise.

It's the newest variation on the story Montana has known for more than a hundred years. Somebody got the shaft then, and somebody gets it now. The cattlemen and gold seekers came in and pushed the Native Americans onto reservations. The homesteaders came in and fenced out the free-range cattle. The engineers dammed rivers and flooded out the homesteaders. The out-of-staters come in and fence out the neighboring townspeople.

Have we learned anything in a century?

Bill and Sarah's Bookstore & Coffeehouse has an eclectic collection of reading materials. You can order an espresso, play Chinese checkers, and pick out your weekend's book.

About thirteen miles up a washboard road (trailers not recommended) is Branham Lakes Campground, at 8,800-feet elevation. It has fine sites, decent fishing, and trailheads that lead you through flowering meadows to the dry ridges atop the Tobacco Roots. It's a perfect place for families.

FOLLOWING THE JEFFERSON
Fishing figures prominently in the pleasant town of Twin Bridges, home of world-famous Winston Rods. The Ruby, Beaverhead, and Big Hole rivers combine nearby to form the Jefferson, so scenic floating opportunities are abundant.

As are fishing guides, fishing lodges, and, of course, fish.

Town is modest and low key. Trendiness hasn't hit yet, although there are a few galleries. The newest place to eat is The Old Hotel—you can't go wrong with Jane Waldie's cooking. The Twin Bridges Historical Association bought the 1917 Reid Building, determined to create a first-class museum to preserve the area's history.

If you're in town on a Saturday morning, get fresh produce at the Farmers Market, held in the Main

John Ellingson prints playbills by hand in Virginia City
BEVERLY R. MAGLEY PHOTO

Street park. Floating Flotillas & Fish Fantasies on a July weekend is great fun. And if you ever wonder who all lives in this area, stay for the Madison County Fair in August. Nobody misses that one.

The highway follows the Jefferson River north, through Silver Star. Silver Star once served the gold miners who worked the Highland Range just west of town. It had the first patented underground gold mine in Montana and was one of the largest towns in the region in the 1870s, but fizzled by 1915 after the gold, silver, and lead played out.

You can't miss Lloyd Harkins' place. He has restored Union Pacific and Great Northern cabooses, and has a yard full of threshers and old mining equipment and parts. You know, parts. Things that only a few people know the uses for anymore. "I just didn't want this old stuff to disappear," he said. Harkins is happy to show people around the place if he's home, so if you're an old-mining-equipment buff, stop by.

Keep your eyes open for sandhill cranes in the fields near the river as you drive to Whitehall. There are several good public campgrounds in the cottonwoods on the river bottom, and the diverse bird life keeps up a fine-tuned racket in the predawn hours. The Jefferson River offers fine floating and tubing on hot summer days.

Whitehall's little-known claim to fame occurs year-round every Sunday afternoon between 3 and 8 p.m. at the Borden Hotel, when families come from as far as Helena and Butte to two-step, waltz, and polka to live music. A few blocks north of the tracks, volunteers have done a truly remarkable task converting the old Sanitary Dairy into the Jefferson Valley Museum. The historical society formed in 1990 for the town's centennial, and their enthusiasm has carried them through digging out two feet of manure from the horse stalls to reroofing the huge structure built in 1914. It's worth a visit just to leaf through the notebook that chronicles how they converted the barn into this museum.

There is no lack of good steak houses in the towns surrounding

AROUND WHITEHALL, DIVERSE BIRD LIFE, INCLUDING SANDHILL CRANES, KEEPS UP A FINE-TUNED RACKET

the Tobacco Roots. In fact, only bars and espresso machines might outnumber the opportunities for a good steak. The LaHood Riverview Inn provides consistently good beef, and weekend floaters can stop there for breakfast or lunch.

Lewis & Clark Caverns (287-3032) is Montana's most popular state park, with good reason. The speleothems, or calcite formations, are fantastic, and guides provide an informative, witty tour. You'll hear locals refer to them as Morrison Caves, a holdover from the 1930s when Dan Morrison ran the tours. For more information on the caverns and three other nearby state parks, see "Travel in Time," *Montana Magazine* March/April 1997.

If you don't come equipped with your own, you can rent canoes at the Canoeing House (285-3488) on Highway 2. Located on the Jefferson River near Three Forks, they'll shuttle your vehicle while you float the Jefferson, Madison, Gallatin, or Missouri.

THREE FORKS
"The Sac," built in 1910 to serve Milwaukee Railroad passengers

Sandhill crane
DONALD M. JONES PHOTO

The Sacajawea Hotel invites relaxation
TIM EGAN PHOTO

and crews, anchors Three Forks' business district. Today the Sacajawea Hotel, open year round, is known for some of the finest dining in Montana, and pleasant, comfortable hotel rooms (800-821-7326). I'm partial to their huckleberry nut halibut, with garlic mashed potatoes and flawlessly-cooked seasonal fresh vegetables. One of my good friends, a self-taught gourmet cook, says that "presentation is everything," but the Sac doesn't just present it beautifully, they follow through with flavor.

The new kid on the block for lodgings is Bud Lilly's Angler's Retreat (285-6690). Bud is a well known fishing outfitter-guide. This is a no-frills boarding house that Bud's mother Violet operated for fifty years. After she passed away, Bud had the place renovated to serve anglers, and today's guests can arrange to meet him and talk fishing, on the river or in the parlor. They can also help themselves to fresh salad greens from the garden out back, or zip up to Wheat Montana's bakery/deli for supplies.

If the fish aren't biting, try the links at Headwaters Golf Course, or mosey into Headwaters Heritage Museum, housed in an old bank building. In 1982, historical society volunteers began to raise donations to pay off the bank's $85,000 purchase and renovation cost. The community rallied, and paid the entire bill in just a year and a half.

The museum has two floors chock-full of displays. My favorite is the barbed wire collection, showing 701 different styles of wire. Who'd ever have guessed?

Located about seven miles from three forks, the Madison River Inn (285-3914) overlooks the braiding lower Madison, rich in wildlife and view of the Tobacco Roots and Madisons. The main house is a bed and breakfast inn and conference center. It's a pleasure to sit on the veranda and watch pelicans, cranes, herons, hawks, geese, ducks, swans...

MADISON RIVER VALLEY
If you want a taste of really-small-town-Montana, drive through

Three Forks past the Luzenac talc plant to Willow Creek, and stop at the Willow Creek Cafe and Saloon. The tin ceiling still retains bullet holes from "the good old days," folks are friendly (and not packing pistols these days), and the burgers and fries are outstanding. Don't leave without a piece of fresh pie. Call ahead (285-3698) to find out when country rock band Montana Rose is playing here. Two of the members live in Willow Creek, as does Michael Myers, another musician.

Willow Creek Gallery and Fly Fishing Center combines works of southwestern Montana artists, hand-tied flies, and a kicked-back attitude. You're welcome to go in and browse and chat.

The back way to Highway 287 is a gorgeous drive through ranching country with views of the Tobacco Roots (look for unmistakable Hollowtop Mountain), the Bridgers, and the Spanish Peaks in the Madisons. Be prudent about choosing this route: the ruts might swallow a passenger car if it has rained or the road crew hasn't been through in a while. Stay on the road intermittently marked Yellowstone Trail, and you'll intersect Highway 287 just north of milepost 78.

Eight miles southwest of Pony, Potosi Campground is a great jump-off for trails into the high peaks of the Tobacco Roots. If you have a backpack, hike up to Bell Lake and camp. From there you can walk atop the ridges between peaks for a 360-degree view that'll knock your socks off. You can see southeast into the high peaks of the Taylor-Hilgard, northeast to the Bridgers, and west across the Ruby, Big Hole, and Jefferson river valleys to the Pioneers. The fishing is pretty good in many of those high lakes, too, but I'm not telling which ones. The joy is in discovery, right?

If you're not into camping, The Lodge at Potosi (685-3594) provides exclusive lodgings and

Hollowtop Mountain is a distinctive peak on east side of the Tobacco Roots
RICK & SUSIE GRAETZ PHOTO

gourmet meals. Guests can fish, ride horses, mountain bike, or hike, and return to soak in beautiful hot springs pools adjacent to a granite cliff. The springs was operated as a resort from 1892 until the 1920s, a favorite of mining moguls from Virginia City, Anaconda, and Butte. The original lodge burned, and a new one was built in 1979. The Trapp family bought it in 1991 and added four cabins. As we walked up the old wagon trace, hopping over moose droppings, Dale Trapp pointed out some of the eighteen cold and hot springs pouring into the creek. Later, we sampled his home-brewed beer: a pale ale, a wheat, a porter, a stout. Outstanding. This is a wonderful mountain retreat. Pricey, but they deliver.

For a much less expensive soak in a natural hot springs, try the one in a cow pasture in Norris. Many places these days claim to be rustic. My dictionary says rustic is, among other things, lacking polish, marked by simplicity, artless, sturdy. Well, Norris Hot Springs is the epitome of rustic. I love it.

A few miles east of Norris, a public boat launch gets you on the lower Madison, which meanders through some amazing birding country. It's mostly flat with a few riffles, but put down your binoculars regularly and be alert for dangerous snags and other hazards. You're almost guaranteed sightings of great blue herons, eagles, mergansers, and Canada geese.

Topping the divide between Norris and McAllister, look just west of the highway for traces of the old Bozeman Trail. The wagon tracks, even after a hundred years, are still easy to pick out on the dry hillside.

Turn off Highway 287 at McAllister if you're prepared to raft or kayak the whitewater stretch of the Madison through Beartrap

Canyon. The Bear Claw Bar & Grill at McAllister is known for good steaks and good times. I like the teriyaki swordfish or the T-bone, especially on nights when the bar has live blues guitar. You can picnic, swim, boat, fish, and camp above the canyon at Ennis Lake. Lakeshore Lodge is situated in the only grove of trees seen for miles. The dirt road to the launch site below the power plant is an interesting trip in itself, as long as you're okay driving a narrow lane with occasional steep dropoffs and no guard rails. The river cuts an interesting gorge through 2.7-billion-year-old gneiss and schist.

Drive west along South Meadow Creek into the Tobacco Roots. It ends at a small, fishable lake. Or try Sureshot Lake, off the North Meadow Creek road, to hike, fish, and camp. Passenger vehicles can drive part way up South Meadow Creek and then descend along Granite Creek to Virginia City. It's an interesting drive, but use a national forest map!

Outback Llamas (587-7964) offers guided day hikes in the Tobacco Roots. It's a fine way to see the mountains without lugging all the gear on your back or wondering if you're getting lost. Their guides can talk about the local history, geology, and natural history, and then produce a great lunch for you. Such a deal!

Ennis caters to people who like to fish. Don't let anybody kid you about all the fish being gone from the Madison. Yes, a percentage of the rainbows have been hit by whirling disease, but at 2,500 trout a mile near Ennis, that still leaves an awful lot of catchable rainbows and browns.

Ennis has been discovered, to be sure. About seventy percent of its economy is based on tourism. Real estate subdivisions litter the area, but citizens are working on a new master plan for development

NORRIS HOT SPRINGS, IN A COW PASTURE, IS THE EPITOME OF RUSTIC. I LOVE IT

in town and the county. There is some advantage to being discovered, of course. The IGA has a surprisingly diverse selection of items. The main street is a pleasant place to stroll, with assorted shops, guide services, and bars. Hungry? Breakfast at the Ennis Pharmacy is always good. For dinner, the Continental Divide Restaurant has a well-deserved statewide reputation for excellence. Or duck in the side door of the Claim Jumper Saloon for Southwestern cuisine at Banditos. I often walk to the back of the Longbranch Saloon for dinner from their un-ordinary menu. Be sure to lead off with their French onion soup—the best in Montana.

After dinner in July and August you can catch a $3 movie ($1.50 for kids) at the theater, and if you linger afterwards maybe strike up a conversation with Jess and Grace Armitage. They have operated the projector and concessions for more than thirty years.

There are guest ranches and fishing lodges, motels, and bed and breakfasts. The Sportsman's Lodge and Restaurant is reliably pleasant. Or head back to Virginia City to stay in one of the places you missed earlier.

There's only one problem with this surf and turf loop around the Tobacco Roots. It's a sure bet you'll want to extend the weekend to a full week. Or two. ✧

Lakes, Links, & Lollygagging

by Brad Hurd

HAVE YOU EVER WONDERED WHERE YOU'D CHOOSE TO LIVE IF YOU WERE UNABLE TO VENTURE MORE THAN a day's drive from that place? For some crazy reason I have. And I usually come up with the same conclusion: Missoula. A good part of my reasoning is all the remarkable adventure that's within just a few hours of that town.

All roads leading from Missoula offer enough recreational opportunity and scenery to fill a lifetime. But my favorite—and I've contemplated and researched this subject most of my adult life—is the route up the Blackfoot River, north through the Seeley-Swan, jog over to Bigfork, then south along the east shore of Flathead Lake, down through the Mission Valley and back to Missoula. You could easily spend an entire summer along this 230-mile loop.

Before you hit the road, consider the gear you may want to take along. Certainly you can't use it all, but equipment you could put to very good summertime use includes a fly rod, canoe, golf clubs, backpack and day pack, rubber raft or float tube, mask, snorkel and flippers, and mountain bike.

Come to think of it, you could use all that equipment—hiking, rafting, fishing, swimming, mountain biking, and playing golf—within twenty minutes of downtown Missoula and never bore yourself, so don't be hasty in departing.

Regatta on Flathead lake
BARBARA THOMAS PHOTO

MISSOULA
For sustenance before a major outing, consider a hearty breakfast at The Shack, the Old Town Cafe, or Goldsmith's. All are easy to find and reasonably priced.

My winner for the Best Recreation Area in a City's Backyard is the Rattlesnake National Recreation Area and Wilderness, a 60,000-acre playground just north of Missoula that accommodates hiking, backpacking, horseback riding, and mountain biking. The main trail, actually an old farm and logging road, parallels Rattlesnake Creek. The gentle grade makes it ideal for kids and older folks. A network of smaller trails enables you to "get lost" within a few minutes of the main trailhead. If you're planning an excursion, buy the Rattlesnake map at the Missoula Ranger District office.

For mountain biking, pedal up the main corridor to Franklin Bridge and beyond. The farther you go, the more spectacular the scenery and abundant the wildlife. It's not rare to see black bears, mountain goats, deer, and elk. Don't ride your bike past the wilderness boundary—they're illegal there. The more ambitious among us trek into the backcountry wilderness to numerous high country lakes.

When you're back in Missoula and want the best view of the city, hike the popular M Trail on the west face of Mount Sentinel. A landmark since 1908, it was assembled by the UM Forestry Club members as a symbol of their school. In 1912, a wood letter replaced the initial stone M. It was blown off the mountain in 1915 and replaced with a bigger, more secure letter. In 1968, the present concrete letter was poured at a cost of $4,328. The M shares the hillsides of Mount Sentinel with very discernible shoreline markings from the ancient Glacial Lake Missoula.

Don't overlook Pattee Canyon Recreation Area southeast of town. It's ideal for an after-work hike and picnic. The picnic facilities were built in the 1930s by the Civilian Conservation Corps. Nearby stand some of the grandest old-growth ponderosa pines in western Montana. The Nez Perce and Salish once traveled through here to avoid attacks by the Blackfeet in nearby Hellgate Canyon.

In Hellgate Canyon, the Kim Williams Nature Trail along the Clark Fork River provides a great morning walk or jog from the downtown hotels or from campus.

Any hike should be rewarded by an ice cream at Goldsmith's, just across the footbridge on the north side of campus. The Missoula Chamber of Commerce, with its abundant local informa-

University of Montana–Missoula campus
RICK GRAETZ PHOTO

tion, is almost next door.

Missoula has several good golf courses. The best are the public Larchmont and the private Missoula Country Club, home to the first sod putting green in Montana.

Don't shortchange the city environs for fly-fishing opportunities. I won't give away any of my secrets, but stop in at any of the local fly shops or sporting goods stores where you'll typically find lots of friendly, unpretentious advice. Beware: They are easy places to spend lots of money. Great stuff!

Don't depart Missoula without soaking up some of the urban color. Stroll across campus, visit the Farmers' Market on the north end of Higgins Avenue Tuesday evenings or Saturday mornings, grab a bite at the Out to Lunch Wednesday extravaganza in Caras Park on the riverfront. While you're there, take a spin on the carousel. The artistry of its thirty-eight hand-carved ponies and two chariots, and the story of how they came to be is truly a marvel. Bring a picnic and blanket to Bonner Park for an evening concert on Wednesdays. Check the *Missoulian* newspaper for other drama, arts, and entertainment options.

Want more? Downtown, grab lunch or picnic supplies at Worden's Market and then visit Rockin' Rudy's, a retail store I won't even try to describe. Just don't miss it.

BLACKFOOT MEANDERS

Drive east on Interstate 90 and exit at Highway 200 toward Great Falls. On your way up along the Blackfoot River, you'll pass through Bonner, an old Anaconda Company town. I like to leave the highway at Johnsrud Park and take the old Ninemile Prairie road that traces the river. It's bumpy and dusty, but worth it. This is superb family river rafting or tubing country, with numerous put-in and take-out spots. Floating from Whitaker Bridge to Johnsrud is an ideal day trip that allows

plenty of time to fish, swim, and picnic as you go. The Blackfoot has remarkably deep holes that are fun to explore with mask and snorkel. Thibadeau Rapids can give you a thrill but usually isn't treacherous.

If you're a ghost town buff, take a side trip off Highway 200 to Garnet, which still has graphic reminders of Montana's gold mining era. A visitor center provides maps and can acquaint you with the rough and tumble life of an 1870s mining camp.

SEELEY-SWAN

Back on Highway 200, turn north at Clearwater Junction onto Highway 83. When you round the corner above Salmon Lake, you'll get the picture of what you're in for in the miles ahead. If there's a prettier chain of lakes than those from Salmon to Swan, please tell me about it on a postcard.

The Double Arrow Ranch near Seeley Lake offers great accommodations and fine dining and is home to a very quaint but tricky nine-hole golf course. The course is so picturesque that I really didn't mind draining the golf balls out of my bag.

The town of Seeley Lake is a good place for food, beverages, and supplies. Seeley Lake (the lake), like most of the bigger lakes along our route, has excellent public campgrounds. It's an ideal

stop for water sports.

The hike to Morrell Falls east of Seeley makes a memorable five-mile round-trip family outing. The trail, moderate and shaded, skirts Morrell Lake before reaching a series of very pretty falls and cascades.

If you canoe, look for the Clearwater Canoe Trail, just off the highway north of Seeley Lake. The Clearwater River, deep and slow-moving, meanders lazily for several miles before feeding into Seeley Lake. Early morning and evening paddles are best and enhance your chances of viewing deer, moose, finches, grebes, ducks, and warblers. The hike back to the put-in is much shorter than you'd think, since the more-direct foot trail takes most of the kinks out of the 3.5-mile canoe trail.

One of the beauties of the Seeley-Swan Valley is that you can't make a wrong turn. All of these glacial lakes are exquisite; all the backroads are worth venturing on for a look around. Include some hours, if not days, in your trip itinerary for exploring. If you need suggestions, stop by the Seeley Lake Ranger Station north of town and pick up a copy of *Seeley Lake Recreation Opportunities.*

Traveling north, lakes Inez and Alva are eye-catching. My two favorite lakes—and, again, you can't go wrong with any of them—are Lindbergh and Holland. At Lindbergh, consider canoeing to a huckleberry patch. In most years, huckleberries abound along the shoreline in late July and into August. If you paddle the length of the lake you can hook up with a trail that takes you to Crystal Lake. This paddling, hiking, and berry-picking trip can make a perfect day.

Hiking in "The Bob"
RICK GRAETZ PHOTO

The Forest Service campgrounds on the north side of Holland Lake are my family's top choice, in part because they have flush toilets and are a short walk to Holland Lake Lodge. Its restaurant provides a nice break from camp cooking. The campgrounds fill up early on weekends and holidays and the lodge and cabins are often booked well in advance, for good reason. Take a minute to enjoy the panorama from the lakeside lawn at the lodge.

Holland Lake Falls trail gets my vote for the Best Two-Hour Family Hike. The cool mist from the falls is a perfect tonic on a hot day. The views across the lake toward the Mission Mountains are astounding, particularly when you're standing in hot sunshine and the peaks are still holding lots of snow. When my kids were little, they really got a kick out of this hike. It'll make young children life-long devotees to the outdoors.

If you like the trek to the falls, you'll really like hiking to Upper Holland Lake. It's far more strenuous and can take most of a day to hike up and back, but this popular entry to the million-acre Bob Marshall Wilderness provides a very convincing explanation of why "The Bob" is one of the most beloved wilderness areas in the nation.

Another hike in a class by itself is the route to Glacier and Turquoise lakes on the Mission Mountains side of the valley. A couple miles north of the Holland Lake turnoff, head west on Route 561. It'll take you the better part of an hour to drive to the trailhead. These lakes are jewels and make my short list of "must hikes." Just as you'll find with a Lindbergh Lake canoe trip, your progress can be slowed to a near standstill from mid-July through August if you have a weakness for hucks.

If you're more confined to a car, you still have plenty of scenic viewing options on the main highway. I always pull off the road at the Swan Peak Scenic Viewpoint between Condon and Swan Lake. Talk about a rest area with a view!

FLATHEAD LAKE AREA

Bigfork is a charming resort town where the Swan River empties into Flathead Lake. If your tour includes cuisine and culture, plan a stopover to sample the excellent restaurants and browse through the unique gift stores. While my

Lake Inez
JOHN LAMBING PHOTO

wife and daughters shop, I like to stroll through the many art galleries, among the best in the Northern Rockies.

This village also is home to the renowned Bigfork Summer Playhouse, which stages performances every night of the week except Sunday. Call ahead (837-4886) for reservations. On Sunday evenings the village hosts the Riverbend Concert Series at Sliter Park. A particularly eventful weekend is the first in August when Bigfork hosts the annual Festival of the Arts, and Antique Wooden Boat Show.

Just west of town is Eagle Bend, a thoughtfully designed golf resort. Among its twenty-seven holes are some of the most memorable and challenging I've played anywhere. Reserving tee times (phone 800-255-5641) is recommended.

There's a good variety of accommodations in and around Bigfork. The local chamber of commerce can help you out. For overnight camping, I like Wayfarer State Park, within walking distance of town. It offers great Flathead Lake swimming from rocky outcrops along the shore.

Wayfarer is another superb sunset-watching spot. Come to think of it, on most every evening of this trip you should find yourselves situated in a lawn chair by a lake at sunset.

The sojourn down the East Shore Highway should be leisurely and, in the latter part of the summer, include a stop at a roadside cherry stand. Yellow Bay—home to the University of Montana's Biological Station, water-quality caretakers for the largest freshwater lake west of the Mississippi—is another good stop for a swim, picnic or overnight camping.

THE RES

The midpoint of Flathead Lake marks the northern boundary of the Flathead Indian Reservation.

The 1.2-million-acre reservation is home to the Confederated Salish and Kootenai tribes, a combination of the Salish, the Pend d'Oreille, and the Kootenai tribes. Be mindful that tribal lands are governed by tribal fish, wildlife and recreation rules and, in some cases, fees. This information is easily accessible throughout the reservation offices.

The town of Polson has a pleasant and affordable eighteen-hole golf course. Its views of Flathead Lake are so mesmerizing that a double-bogey can be shrugged off...well, almost. Make note of the old log clubhouse. Now called the Clubhouse Theater, it hosts summer productions of the Port Polson Players.

Polson's Riverside Park is on the west edge of town where the outflow from the lake forms the Flathead River. Nearby is the stylish, tribally-owned lakeside resort called KwaTaqNuk, which means "where the water leaves the lake." It's a great place for lunch on the deck, and it rents boats and wave runners.

Many folks make a beeline from Polson to Missoula, bypassing some unique wildlife, cultural, and scenic offerings. The Ninepipes National Wildlife Refuge is a birdwatcher's paradise. The wetlands there seem to have a pact going with the Mission Mountains when it comes to reflecting the mountains' brilliance in the water.

Near Pablo, The People's Center can acquaint you with tribal culture. It offers an exhibit gallery, Native EdVentures tours, and educational programs.

There's more very good golf just west of Ronan, if you haven't gotten your fill.

At St. Ignatius, visit the mission. Built in 1854 by Native Americans under the direction of Catholic missionaries, it contains fifty-eight murals on the walls and ceiling. Native American culture,

NATIONAL BISON RANGE SELF-GUIDED AUTO TOUR MEANS VIEWING MANY WILD ANIMALS

crafts, and artifacts are displayed in St. Ignatius at the Four Winds Historic Village and the Flathead Indian Museum.

Take a detour off Highway 93 to the National Bison Range at Moiese. The self-guided auto tour is very worthwhile for wildlife viewing and a spectacular vantage of the Mission Range and Valley. About 500 bison roam the nearly 20,000 acres of natural grassland, along with deer, elk, bighorn sheep, pronghorn antelope, and numerous songbirds.

On your way back into Missoula, swing by the airport west of town and tour the Smokejumpers Center to experience the lore and technology of forest fire-fighting. Continuing into town on Broadway, there's the Rocky Mountain Elk Foundation wildlife visitors center, a must for elk enthusiasts.

If you land back in town at dinnertime, good choices abound. My favorites include The Depot (steak and seafood), the Alleycat Grill (gourmet), The Mustard Seed (contemporary Oriental), and Zimorino's (Italian).

You might allow a little extra time in town to finish up some of the things you couldn't get to at the beginning of the trip. Or better yet, come again another time. As I said, there's a lifetime of adventure to be found on the roads leading out of Missoula. ✧

AUTUMN

History, Horizons, & Hi-Line

by T. J. Gilles

THE NORTH COUNTRY OUT OF GREAT FALLS PROVIDES OPEN-AIR HISTORY OPPORTUNITIES PERHAPS unmatched in this neck of the plains. To the northeast on Highway 87, Fort Benton boasts of being the birthplace of Montana and in the summer of 1996 celebrated its 150th year of settlement. To the northwest there are dinosaur digs and the Old North Trail used thousands of years ago by emigrants who walked overland across what is now the Bering Strait to inhabit all of the Americas.

Before leaving Great Falls to embark on this 300-mile history lesson, some reading beforehand would help enrich the journey. Try fiction: A.B. Guthrie, Jr.'s *The Big Sky* is essential reading about the fur trade; Ivan Doig's Rocky Mountain Front novels, especially *English Creek,* bring life to generations of Montana history; James Welch's *Fools Crow* tells of settler-Indian conflicts of a century or more ago in the country you'll be traveling through.

For more visual pre-trip research, start at the C. M. Russell Museum in Great Falls. Russell's paintings bring to life much of the history involving Indian and cowboy days, including the first meetings between indigenous peoples and the fringe representatives of European culture and commerce, such as explorers

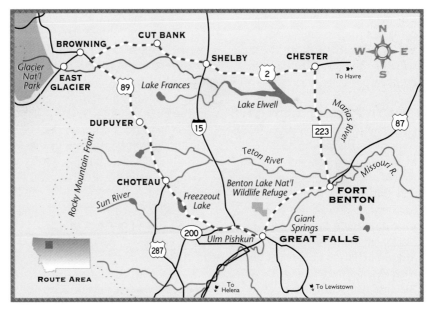

(including Lewis and Clark), fur trappers, the military, and freighters. The Russell paintings also provide the mind's eye with many of the landscapes you'll encounter during the weekend's exploration, such as the oft-pictured Square Butte, the Rocky Mountain Front, and the Missouri Breaks.

The most arduous portion of

the 1804-1806 Lewis and Clark expedition was the month-long summer portage through sagebrush and prickly pear, across the grizzly-infested plains around the Great Falls of the Missouri. The Corps of Discovery crossed through what now is the city of Great Falls.

Before taking off on this weekend sweep, remember: Fort Ben-

FACING PAGE: *Ulm Pishkun and Square Butte* JOHN LAMBING PHOTO

PRECEDING PAGE: *Fishing the Bighorn River* PAUL UPDIKE PHOTO

ton attractions are open on Sundays; most attractions in Choteau, Browning, Cut Bank, Shelby, and Chester are open from late morning to late afternoon, Tuesdays through Saturdays only, during the fall off-season.

To set the tone and start the day outdoors, walk or bike the River's Edge Trail out to Giant Springs State Park, or drive to the Ulm Pishkun south of Great Falls, just off Interstate 15. The pishkun is a mile-long expanse of sandstone cliffs used thousands of years ago by Indians who stampeded herds of bison to their deaths. Some archaeologists say it may prove to be the largest buffalo jump in the world. The pishkun cliffs—and Square Butte in the background—often are spectacular in the early morning or evening twilight, as many a Russell painting will attest.

A new interpretive center is being built below the bluffs, but a walk from above down the trail remains the most personal interpretation.

FAIRFIELD BENCH

From the pishkun, return to Great Falls and head for the Rocky Mountain Front. Stay on I-15 for twelve miles north of Great Falls and exit at Vaughn on Highway 89 toward Choteau. For about nine miles, you'll be on the old Mullan Road, built in 1862-64 to link the wharves of Fort Benton with U.S. military operations at Walla Walla, Washington, then the head of navigation leading to the Pacific Ocean.

The Fairfield Bench, part of the Greenfields Irrigation Project, is a hub of agricultural activity throughout spring and summer, but quiets down in the fall after

Giant Springs State Park along the Missouri River near Great Falls
RICK & SUSIE GRAETZ PHOTO

the crops are in. Known as the "Malting Barley Capital of the USA," Fairfield is a company town: Anheuser-Busch. That company contracts with area farmers to grow the barley very likely served (in liquid form) at those farmers' own get-togethers.

Irrigation on the bench was expanded in the 1930s as one of many resettlement programs of F.D.R.'s New Deal. Farmers who had lost it all on dryland homesteads entered a lottery for a chance to acquire a piece of land irrigated by the waters stored behind Gibson Dam, named for Great Falls founder Paris Gibson.

Birdwatchers will find it worthwhile to stop at Freezeout Lake, a wildlife area that swarms each spring and fall with hundreds of thousands of waterfowl stopping by during their migrations from as far north as the Arctic tundra to as far south as Central America. If you're there on a peak day—such as when 100,000 white tundra swans are congregated—it's the sight of a lifetime.

Depending on when you arrive in the fall, it may be hunting season, and duck and goose hunters might be stalking in the cattails and sedge. But there is a good, safe viewing area near the highway.

CHOTEAU

From Freezeout, it's on to Choteau in Teton County, with the three

crosses on Priest Butte to the left announcing that you're almost to the outskirts. Choteau is a must stop. Choteau the town and adjoining Chouteau County (Fort Benton is the seat), although spelled differently, are named for members of the Chouteau family, French traders originally from New Orleans who also have streets and boulevards named for them in St. Louis, where their early fur-trading enterprises were headquartered, and in Kansas City, which they founded.

Choteau is known for Egg Mountain, where digs by Jack Horner of the Museum of the Rockies in Bozeman resulted in new theories about dinosaurs and how they raised their young. The Old Trail Museum complex on the northwest end of town shouldn't be missed. Standing guard are life-sized replicas of dinosaurs that once ruled the earth, as well as more modern relics such as a printing press and a linotype machine. One of the more unusual displays is the actual skeleton of an early pioneer, including the arrow points that killed him. Fossils and fool's gold are on sale dirt cheap.

In the complex is a reconstructed Métis cabin, complete with homemade crafts and musical instruments. Along with Lewistown, Choteau was one of the centers of Métis settlement in Montana in the 19th century.

Wheat field along the Rocky Mountain Front
JOHN LAMBING PHOTO

Famous for their squeaking Red River carts, the Métis ("mixed blood") were of French and Native American ancestry and combined elements of both cultures. Many lived in log-cabin settlements and played traditional music from their French heritage, but also roamed each year to take part in communal buffalo hunts.

For the past few years, a local group, Métis Cultural Recovery, Inc., has worked to create more awareness of the Métis civilization. French folklorists have discovered that many ancient songs thought to have been lost for centuries have been kept alive in Montana and Western Canada. Louis Riel, the visionary who was executed for leading a rebellion when he sought to establish a Métis homeland in Canada a century ago, taught near Choteau and at St. Peter's Mission near Cascade, prior to launching his plot. One Métis colony thrived about thirty miles west of town near Pine Butte, and a new Bureau of Land Management trail skirts a Métis cemetery near Ear Mountain, where *The Big Sky* author A.B. Guthrie, Jr. lived. One of Montana's premier journalists and historians, Joseph Kinsey Howard, died near Choteau while completing his Riel biography, the gripping *Strange Empire*.

Choteau features several good eateries on Main Street, an ice cream store within the Old Trail complex, and the Outpost Deli across the street from the dinosaurs. A favorite eating and socializing spot is the Log Cabin Cafe, a restaurant and deli on the southeast end of town across from the sandstone courthouse. The roof is adorned by covered wagons and inside there's a mixture of local cattlemen and farmers, visiting hunters and mountain climbers, and high school kids hanging out and having a shake.

Along the Front, dude ranching and bed-and-breakfast facilities are few and far between. Examples are the H Lazy 6 Fly Fishing Lodge twenty miles west of Choteau, with its stocked trout ponds and gourmet dining, and the Styren Ranch Guest House, eight miles north of town on Highway 89.

ALONG THE FRONT
Hit the highway north, and check out the Rose Room in Pendroy. They have good food and irreverent ambiance, symbolized by the fake fire hydrant on Main Street.

Back on 89, it's another twenty-two miles to the junction with Highway 44, heading east to

Valier and Lake Frances' boating and camping facilities. The lake is well stocked with walleye, northern pike, and yellow perch. If it's a Saturday and you've never seen an eight-man high school football game, find out if the Valier Panthers are having a home game.

Farther north near the Two Medicine River, those wishing an intensive history lesson can get one through Blackfeet cultural leader Curly Bear Wagner. His guided, off-road tours ($50 per person half-day, $100 all day), visit such archaeological sites as Old Agency, the mission, Ghost Ridge, and tipi rings.

From Valier, head to Browning and attractions such as the Museum of the Plains Indian, and Bob Scriver's Studio Museum of Wildlife and Hall of Bronze. The Museum of the Plains Indian is one of just four federally assisted Indian museums. Exhibits include historic clothing, tools, and weapons. Its museum store offers Indian-made arts and crafts, ceremonial sweetgrass braids, and reproductions of art produced by Native Americans, many with solid international reputations.

THE HI-LINE
A half-hour east of Browning, Cut Bank's Glacier County Museum includes Indian displays, but oil is king here. Outdoors is the original oilpatch shack once inhabited by Hugo "The Galloping Swede" Aronson during an interlude between the time he jumped off a freight train in Glacier County and when he became governor of Montana. Along with a railroad exhibit, this museum on East Main includes an original cable oil rig and all of the buildings that went with it, as well as a restored one-room schoolhouse.

Shelby is an excellent place for an overnighter, with its variety of restaurants and clubs and an ever-increasing number of motel rooms developing on the west end of the oil city. One of the newer facilities is the Crossroads Inn, where the hallways are adorned with posters advertising movies with "Montana" in the title (but often featuring scenery more like that of the Southwest). Among the restaurants downtown, my favorites include surf and turf entrees at the Sports Club or Chinese cuisine at Chan's. A transportation hub on the Burlington Northern Santa Fe Railroad, Shelby's rail yards are busy. Its transloader facility piggybacks trailers onto flatbed railcars and it's an Amtrak stop for passengers headed east or west. Trains roll through day and night.

Known for its night life since the speakeasy days, on any Friday or Saturday night downtown Shelby is likely to have several bands playing anything from punk rock to country and western. Hogan's Tap Room won't have a band, but it does house the bell used during the 1923 Dempsey-Gibbons heavyweight championship fight in Shelby. Ring the bell, buy a round. Read Deidre McNamer's novel *One Sweet Quarrel*.

The Marias Museum in Shelby celebrates the oil industry, coal and gold mining in the Sweetgrass Hills, the livestock and farming industries, and Native Americans.

Tipis in Heart Butte on the Blackfeet Indian Reservation
KERRY T. NICKOU PHOTO

54

Marias River along the Hi-Line
JOHN LAMBING PHOTO

The big draw, of course, is memorabilia from the Dempsey-Gibbons fight.

For an unusual side trip out of Shelby by day, head about sixteen miles north on I-15 to view some latter-day history. Leave the freeway at the Four Corners exit to Kevin, Oilmont, Ferdig. The countryside just a few miles east on the paved road is strewn with oilpatch equipment and camp barracks and other petroleum paraphernalia that dates back to the early boom years of the 1920s.

When oil prices rise enough, many of these ancient, creaking cable rigs come back to life to strip a few barrels more out of the Kevin-Sunburst Field. Kevin has the abandoned Old West refinery. Refineries near Cut Bank, Shelby, and Sunburst (where the high school teams are called the Refiners) have long been out of use.

Driving east on Highway 2, you'll pass the drying-up homestead towns of Dunkirk, Devon, Galata, and Lothair (don't blink). The Liberty County Museum in Chester specializes in homestead-era artifacts, and the Liberty County Village Arts Center and Gallery has rotating art exhibits and a variety of art for sale. Stop for lunch or dinner at the Red Onion, or head south on Highway 223 toward Fort Benton.

You'll be in the vicinity of several historic trails. The Whoop-Up Trail north out of Fort Benton took wagonloads of whiskey and other, drier goods to Canadian Indians—prompting tribal requests that resulted in the formation of the Northwest Mounted Police to quell the trade. There's also the Bootlegger Trail, that nocturnal Roaring Twenties flivver run around the Sweetgrass Hills that brought Prohibition-era Canadian spirits into garages in Great Falls and Black Eagle.

FORT BENTON

Fort Benton is worth some time. The Fort Benton Museum on the levee near the old fort and the Montana Agriculture Museum and Center are open on Sundays. The ever-growing ag museum, founded in the mid-1980s, spreads across several acres and includes indoor displays depicting the homesteaders' progress and agricultural technology advances, as well as the famous Hornaday Buffalo once displayed at the Smithsonian.

Outside, organizers are reconstructing a homestead-era town. Ingredients so far include a church (site of several weddings already), blacksmith shop, grain elevator and track siding with railcars, bank, and other buildings. Larger pieces of farm equipment, some of it in various stages of restoration, are inside and out.

Downtown, the city park's lawn covers the grounds of the original Fort Benton, established by fur traders in 1846. An old blockhouse and a few walls are all that remain of the original adobe compound, although interpretive signs describe what was where during the trading post's heyday. Volunteers have constructed a fort trading building, and there are plans for more reconstructions.

Methodical archaeological digs continue each year. The museum adjacent to the fort describes the history, including Fort Benton's reign as "Bloodiest Block in the West" when dozens of steamships tied up at the levee to unload foodstuffs and dry (and wet) goods while awaiting the arrival of bullwhacker-driven caravans of gold from Last Chance Gulch.

A walk along the levee from the museum to the Grand Union hotel passes the statues of Lewis, Clark, and Sacajawea, the replica keelboat *Mandan* constructed for filming Guthrie's *The Big Sky*, and a statue of Shep, the dog who waited faithfully for every train at Fort Benton in the 1930s, looking for the return of his deceased master.

Historic homes such as the I.G. Baker residence may be visited, and signs along the levee describe the interesting, often tumultuous history of this now-peaceful town. Characters such as Madam Mustache and territorial acting governor Thomas Francis Meagher (who stepped off a boat and drowned here) made the place interesting.

You might also see anglers and floaters on the river, or stroll the well lighted old bridge down by the fire station to get a better view of the river.

From Fort Benton it's forty-four miles down Highway 87 back to Great Falls. ✧

Pictographs, Prairies, & Peaks

by Katherine Shandera

YOU HAVE TO MAKE A TOUGH DECISION RIGHT OFF THE BAT: SHOULD YOU STAY IN TOWN OR GO ELSEWHERE? This 325-mile route that starts and ends in Billings offers a wealth of things to do. The city's restaurants, theaters, museums, and shops are regional magnets. Weekends are packed with special events. There's hiking, biking, and birdwatching on the Rims and in Riverfront and Two Moon parks, and fishing the Yellowstone.

Mull over the choices during a breakfast of Billings' own Cream of the West hot cereal at Stella's Kitchen and Bakery downtown.

If the road is calling, this route will take you off the main roads and onto the region's less traveled byways. Most of it is on excellent paved roads, across mountains and plains, badlands and sacred lands, coulees and canyons, dry creeks and mighty rivers.

PICTOGRAPH CAVE

A perfect first stop is just seven miles south of town. Take Lockwood exit #452 off I-90 in Billings. Follow the signs to Pictograph Cave State Park. Tucked snugly in a sandstone-rimmed box canyon are three shallow caves overlooking the Bitter Creek and Yellowstone River valleys.

Here, long before the arrival

Playing with the wind atop the Beartooth Plateau
R. VALENTINE ATKINSON PHOTO

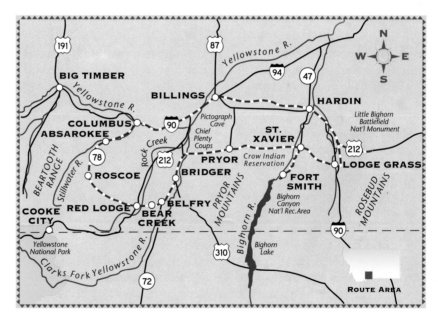

of the Crow, Cheyenne, and Sioux, prehistoric peoples lived, worked, and recorded their stories. Their drawings, together with some from the 1800s, cover the back wall of Pictograph Cave. There are at least 160 drawings, but only a few of the images are visible from the public viewing area. To better understand what's there, ask the park ranger to show

you a tracing of the pictographs. One pictograph dates back at least 3,500 years! To check hours of operation for Pictograph State Park, call 245-0227.

HARDIN

Back at the Lockwood exchange, head east to Hardin via old Highway 87. To find your way out of town, follow the signs for Chief

57

Billings
ERIC E. CHRISTIANSEN PHOTO

Plenty Coups State Park. The narrow two-lane road twists and turns through the rugged hills south of Billings for about 14 miles, then cuts across open prairies and farmland for the remaining 30 miles to Hardin. (Stay on Highway 87 rather than turning toward Chief Plenty Coups State Park at Pryor Creek Road.)

Before Interstate 90 was complete, Highway 87 was the main route into and out of Billings from the southeast. The Fly family's ranch along the highway was so besieged by travelers looking for gas, food, or something to drink that they opened the Fly Inn, a cafe and gas station. It operated from 1929 until 1958. The Fly Inn's old gas station is now part of the historical museum in Hardin.

The Big Horn County Historical Museum on the south edge of Hardin is also a state visitor's center and the place to ask for directions or advice about local roads and attractions. The museum encompasses a 24-acre collection of early-1900s buildings that reflect life for the area's white settlers.

Hardin has a variety of restau-rants ranging from fast-food chains near I-90 to locally owned family-style restaurants like the Purple Cow, the Lariat Cafe, and the Merry Mixer. There are several moderately priced motels. Afi-cionados of bed and breakfast inns will enjoy the historic Becker Hotel or the Kendrick House Inn. The Kendrick House was built as a boarding house near the turn of the 20th century. Modern-day guests may also enjoy the attached antique shop and tea house.

LITTLE BIGHORN BATTLEFIELD

Fifteen miles south of Hardin on I-90 is the exit for the Little Bighorn Battlefield. Hundreds of Indian warriors defeated General George Armstrong Custer and the 7th Cavalry here in 1876. Plan to spend two to four hours. Standing on the battlefield, seeing the remains of shallow trenches dug by the besieged soldiers on Reno Hill, viewing battle artifacts, and hearing the stories passed down by survivors on both sides will make you care about the fate of these soldiers and warriors far more than you ever thought you would.

Battlefield hours change with the seasons, so it's best to check with park headquarters at 638-2621. (History buffs may also want to visit two privately owned museums, the Custer Battlefield Museum and the Reno-Benteen Battlefield Museum, located a few miles south of the Battlefield off the I-90 Garryowen exit.)

Just across the highway from the battlefield is the Custer Battle-field Trading Post and Cafe. Taste a delicious regional specialty, Indian fry bread, there or in the cafe at the bottom of the hill.

Nearby is the new Crow/North-ern Cheyenne Hospital that dis-plays a collection of Crow and Northern Cheyenne artwork and crafts. Also in this area is the Little Bighorn Casino and Restau-rant, owned by the Crow Tribe.

Little Big Horn College runs the bus tours of the battlefield. The college also offers other guided tours, lectures, and presen-tations on Crow culture. Informa-tion about these programs is available at the battlefield visitor's center or at the college, which can be reached from I-90's Crow Agency exit. Phone Little Big Horn College at 638-2621.

LODGE GRASS

Drive 20 miles south on old High-way 87 through the valley of the Little Bighorn River. The best bet for food in Lodge Grass is Steven-son's grocery store. The deli and bakery there make it easy to put together a fast meal.

Leave Lodge Grass via Highway 463 west. About four miles out of town turn right (northwest) on the Good Luck Road, a paved highway that will take you through the Rotten Grass Creek valley to Highway 313, four miles south of St. Xavier.

BIGHORN CANYON

A left turn (south) on Highway 313 will take you along the Big Horn River to Fort Smith, Yellowtail Dam, and the Bighorn Canyon National Recreational Area. The Bighorn River is blue-ribbon trout water that attracts anglers from all over the world. Numerous guides and outfitters are located along the river from Hardin to Fort Smith.

Yellowtail Dam and the Visitor's Center are located a short drive outside Fort Smith. During the summer season, visitors can learn about the dam's construction and take an elevator deep inside to tour its power generation plant.

An 11-mile drive south from the dam to Ok-a-beh (pronounced Okabay) marina provides a much better look at the spectacular canyon reservoir created by the dam. Many people trophy fish in the canyon reservoir, but the views lure even the staunchest fisherman into reverie.

Anchored in the deep blue-green water are miles of towering red rock walls rising hundreds of feet above the water. Once you catch this glimpse of the 71-mile-long canyon, you'll want to see more, and the only way to do that from here is by boat. If you didn't bring your own, the marina offers outboard and pontoon rentals by the hour or the day from May through mid-September.

PRYOR AREA

On the road again, head north back to St. Xavier. This little community was established by Jesuit missionaries in 1887. The original church is still in use and visitors are welcome.

Take the only highway west out of St. Xavier toward Pryor, 44 miles away. The road follows the general route of the Bozeman trail through this area. Near mileposts 21 and 23, stop and try to spot the wagon wheel ruts on the north side of the highway.

After climbing out of the Bighorn River valley, you'll notice acres of cultivated land. From 1917 to 1966, this land was leased and farmed by a white man named Thomas Campbell. His winter wheat operation covered 95,000 acres here in the heart of the Crow Reservation and it was heralded as the world's largest wheat farm. The blacksmith shop

Little Bighorn Battlefield
R. VALENTINE ATKINSON PHOTO

in the museum in Hardin came from Campbell's operation.

Closer to Pryor the landscape changes around every bend. You'll leave the high plains, weave through badlands, drop into wooded canyons, then find yourself back in farmland.

On the west side of Pryor is Chief Plenty Coups State Park. Chief Plenty Coups was a visionary Crow leader who foresaw the powerful forces the Euro-American people would bring and counseled his people, "With education you are the white man's equal, without it, you are his victim." Plenty Coups' wisdom and eloquence were respected around the world and the Crow people so revered him that they declared him the last chief of the Crows. The museum here is the only one devoted solely to Crow culture. For information on park and visitor center hours, call 252-1289.

When leaving Chief Plenty Coups Park, take a right turn onto the gravel road at the entrance and head west toward Edgar. This 15-mile stretch is a good all-weather route that will take you off the reservation and down into the scenic farming and ranching communities of the Clark's Fork Valley.

At Edgar, turn south on Highway 310. As you wend your way closer to the jagged peaks of the Beartooth Mountains, you'll find several attractive roadside picnic areas.

RACING PIGS

Fifteen miles south of Edgar, take the Cody fork of the road (Highway 72) to Belfry. From Belfry, drive Highway 308, clearly marked as the route to Red Lodge.

Almost immediately out of Belfry you leave farmlands and drive through rugged foothills pasturelands. The little commu-

Yellowtail Dam and Reservoir
VICTOR H. COLVARD PHOTO

nity of Bearcreek is the home of the mildly famous Bearcreek Saloon and Bearcreek Downs. This is where hundreds of locals, a few traveling celebrities, and some national news shows come to eat steak and take in Montana's finest thoroughbred pig races. The fleet-footed porkers race every summer weekend. (Iguanas fill in for the pigs during the off season.) For race and chow times call (406) 446-3881.

Just outside of Bearcreek is a historical marker pointing out the old Smith Mine. In 1943, 74 miners died as a result of an explosion there. You can learn more about the Smith Mine from displays at the Bearcreek Saloon or at the historical museum in Red Lodge.

Don't miss the scenic turnout just past Washoe. Unless you can sprout wings, there aren't many chances in life to savor a view like this. After you've distilled the meaning of life, you can pop over the hill to historic, picturesque Red Lodge.

RED LODGE

During peak summer and winter months the streets of Red Lodge buzz with activity. With good reason. Red Lodge boasts fine hotels, gourmet dining, charming little stores, antique shops, and a full calendar of special events. When you're shopping, be sure to check out Sylvan Peaks and Crazy Creek outlets, local enterprises that manufacture quality sporting goods. Crazy Creek's portable chairs are popular nationwide.

Red Lodge is said to have the most restaurants per capita of any city in the state. Even better, almost all of them provide excellent food and service. You could spend several weekends just indulging your tastebuds. For starters, try Bogart's at 11 S. Broadway or Greenlee's at the Pollard Hotel.

If stepping back in time appeals to you, add your name to a list of guests at the Pollard that includes Buffalo Bill, Calamity Jane, General Nelson A. Miles, William Jennings Bryant, and Liver Eatin' Johnson. Recent renovations to the 100-year-old Pollard restore the building's historic character while adding amenities like in-room whirlpool baths.

The power behind Red Lodge's shops, restaurants, and hotels is the abundant outdoor recreation in the area. Whether you want to drive, hike, bike, fish, or ski, Red Lodge is the place to start. The Red Lodge Chamber of Commerce at the north end of town can provide information on options and point you in the right directions. The *Red Lodge Visitors Guide* is loaded with valuable tips for enjoying the area.

THE GREAT OUTDOORS

Near Red Lodge, several easily accessible roads offer striking views as well as hiking and cross-country skiing trails. The Beartooth Highway leading southwest to Cooke City is the most famous and most heavily traveled scenic drive. For less well known routes and trails get a Forest Service map at their office located on the south edge of Red Lodge.

The West Fork of Rock Creek is popular for hiking, biking, and cross-country skiing. A particularly beautiful trail at the end of West Fork Road leads to Quinnebaugh Meadows by way of Sentinel Falls and Calamity Falls. It's a two- to three-hour hike from the trailhead to the meadows.

When you're ready to leave Red Lodge, take Highway 78 northwest toward Roscoe and

Dancer at Crow Fair
R. VALENTINE ATKINSON PHOTO

> UNLESS YOU CAN SPROUT WINGS, THERE AREN'T MANY CHANCES AT VIEWS LIKE THE WASHOE TURNOUT'S

Absarokee. In the summer and early fall this area offers postcard-perfect scenery, with lots of places to picnic, camp, and hike. Jewel-like East Rosebud Lake is reached from a gravel road that runs south out of Roscoe. Three hiking trails at the lake range from easy walking to nearly vertical.

For more mountain majesty, drive Highway 78 past Roscoe to the intersection with Highway 419. At Fishtail, you'll have another choice to make. Highway 425 goes up East Rosebud Creek to a trail leading to Mystic Lake. Staying on 419 takes you through Nye to the Woodbine campground and trailhead on the Stillwater River. This trail offers instant drama. Within minutes of leaving your car, you're on a wide ledge in a steep canyon. A sheer rock wall rises on one side and the churning, roaring river races past on the other.

After all this appetite-building hiking, hit the Grizzly Bar and Restaurant in Roscoe, one of the area's most popular eateries. The food is delicious—a perfect end to a day in the mountains.

With your belly satisfied, savor driving along the Stillwater and Yellowstone river valleys back to Billings. Take Highway 78 north through Absarokee and Columbus, then I-90 east to Billings. While enjoying the views, make a note to arrange a raft trip down the Stillwater or Yellowstone.

You know you're coming back. ✧

Foliage, Farms, & Forests

by Elizabeth and Wilbur Wood

THIS 370-MILE SPIN AROUND THE CENTER OF MONTANA BEGINS IN A THREE-PRONGED RIVER VALLEY cradled against the Beartooth Mountains. South of that cradle lies Yellowstone National Park. North, the country opens into a broad valley of rolling grasslands, wheat fields, and pine ridges. You'll ride the edge between high plains and mountains, circling an "island range"— the Snowy Mountains—and touch down in Montana's geographic center, Lewistown.

BOULDER RIVER COUNTRY

Saturday morning, slide out of bed upstairs in the restored Grand Hotel in Big Timber, which has one of the finest eating and drinking establishments along the Yellowstone River. On a clear morning, you can stroll out onto McLeod Avenue and gaze north at the shining spires and shadowed canyons of the Crazy Mountains.

Big Timber is a friendly community with lots of guest ranches nearby and just a bit of the freeway glint in its eye. All along the Yellowstone River, I-90 seems to add a dash of "here today, gone tomorrow," hollowing out traditional Montana towns as people speed into Billings to buy everything from clothes to computers. Big Timber has a few shops, antiques stores, movie theater, and a good soda foundation at

Coles Drug where you can get a Green River soda or (our favorite) a double-chocolate ice cream soda.

Two galleries are worth noting. Cabin Creek Studio shows wonderful bronze sculptures of wildlife, Indians, and other Western subjects. You may ask for a tour of the foundry. Crazy Mountain Art and Antiques offers a wide selection of furniture, paintings, and assorted goodies in all price ranges.

The Crazy Mountain Museum, open 1-4 p.m. Tuesdays through Sundays, has a fine miniature replica of Big Timber before the 1907 fire. The Shiloh Sharps Rifle factory displays exquisite breech loading rifles in their reception area. They

manufacture replicas of Sharps rifles, and groups can call ahead to arrange a tour.

Drive out of town up the Boulder River, south on narrow Highway 298, sometimes rough and winding, toward McLeod. Cotton-

The Boulder River Valley, south of Big Timber
LARRY MAYER PHOTO

63

woods, willows, and various streamside bushes burn in autumn yellows and reds as you pass sheep and cattle ranches, and the newer horse ranchettes—a sign that the Boulder River may be the next "hot" place along the Beartooth Front now that the Paradise Valley south of Livingston has been colonized by numerous writers, artists, and movie actors. The Boulder River road dead ends in the Gallatin National Forest, at the edge of the Absaroka-Beartooth Wilderness and the Beartooth Plateau, a massive mineral-rich block of igneous rock that surfaced about fifty million years ago. The Boulder Valley has lots of hiking trails and a number of guest ranches, such as McLeod Resort, sixteen miles south of Big Timber. Bring warm clothes for chilly fall nights.

You can camp in the national forest at one of the numerous developed campgrounds. We prefer the middle Boulder area. Avoid the East Boulder campsite, which is surrounded by stumps and slash piles from one of several recent clearcuts, and where views are marred by new power poles leading to a platinum mine being developed farther up the valley. Don't miss the impressive waterfall and natural bridge scenic gorge ten miles south of McLeod. There are clearly marked trails, a sturdy bridge, and informative displays on landscape, geology, and wildlife.

Before leaving the Boulder River area, stop for a beer and a hoagie sandwich—and a look at the bear skin on the wall behind the bandstand—at the McLeod Bar and Roadkill Cafe.

Natural Bridge Scenic Area on the Boulder River, in the Absaroka Range
TIM EGAN PHOTO

YELLOWSTONE RIVER VALLEY

Head back into Big Timber, then let the Yellowstone River's flaring yellow cottonwoods draw you downriver toward Billings.

Just twenty-two miles east of Big Timber, Reedpoint's sign informs you that ninety-six people live there and advertises the town's annual "sheep drive" on Labor Day weekend. Initiated in 1989 as a sheep rancher's joking response to the highly-hyped Montana Centennial Cattle Drive from Roundup to Billings, the annual three-block-long sheep drive down Main Street is now a celebrated event that also raises money for community projects. Both bars in Reedpoint are worth a visit, and one of them is a gem of a bed and breakfast place called the Montana Hotel. Impeccably restored by Russ and Connie Schlievert—tin ceilings from Livingston and Butte, the ornate back of the bar from nearby Grey-cliff—the Montana Hotel has five beautiful rooms, complete with period costumes, available for modest rates, and the Schlieverts plan to offer a full dining menu (phone 326-2288).

Back on and then off the freeway at Columbus, where a barn-like building contains Apple Village: a restaurant (good milk-shakes and sandwiches) and antiques. Nearby is Old West Angler and Outfitters, a friendly fly fishing/outdoor sports shop. You can camp and fish at Itch-Kep-Pe Park on the river, or just picnic at shady tables outside the Montana Silversmiths offices. You're welcome to go inside and see their fine work on display.

Columbus is a good launch point to get into the mountains, up Highway 78 to Absarokee, Red Lodge, and then the Beartooth Highway to Yellowstone Park. You can float the Yellowstone or kayak the Stillwater—a number of outfitters are available to help.

In Laurel, you can poke through antiques and second hand stores, and when the afternoon gets hot, head to the Caboose Saloon & Casino for a Montana style bar with exceptional life-size bronzes on display. Laurel Herbstfest comes late in September, a German harvest celebration with food and drink.

BILLINGS

You could spend days in Billings, the biggest city in Montana, but we will mention only a few highlights to get you started. Interested in history? The Western Heritage Center and the Moss Mansion are fine places to start. Or tour the ancient pictograph caves just southeast of Billings. Coffeehouses and galleries are downtown, each with its own flavor. Our choices are Todd's Plantation, Cafe Jones, Artspace, and the McCormick Cafe. Walker's Grill and Juliano's are exceptional eating establishments. Pug Mahon's, Casey's Golden Pheasant, and The Rex are great pubs. Picnic and a walk? Try an afternoon at ZooMontana, enjoy the Scent Garden, the Siberian tigers, birds by the creek, ducks on the pond. Atop the rimrocks you can look out over this flashy town. Highrises and smokestacks are prominent, but in autumn the trees are spectacular and at night the city glitters electric. On a clear day the Bighorn, Pryor, and Beartooth ranges fill the southern horizon.

HIGH PLAINS

Highway 87 moves north onto the high plains toward the Bull Mountains that form the divide between the Yellowstone and Musselshell rivers. The Bulls are here because of coal and fire. Ancient lightning-caused fires ignited coal seams that simmered to form clinkers harder than the surrounding Fort Union sandstone, and kept these hills from eroding as fast as the plains around them.

Yet another town abandoned by the railroad and Old Man Coal, Roundup has rebounded and is developing a character of its own. Near the fairgrounds by the river is good camping under the cottonwoods in the Cowbelles Corral. It's free, but donations are encouraged.

This town of 2,400 may have more coffee shops per capita than even Billings. Best bets: 119 Main, which also markets tasteful gifts, and Blue Star Espresso, with its

sandwiches and soups.

Across Main, Bull Mountain Trading is the most interesting among the town's several second-hand, antiques, and crafts stores. The Busy Bee Cafe has a salad bar and a good Mexican omelette. Stella's is the place for steaks. The Grand Bar, for sandwiches, a variety of beers, big screen TV, and a classic rock and country jukebox and dance floor. The walls of the Pioneer Cafe feature some historical photographs. A fine local historical museum (open May through September) explores the area's ranching, homesteading, and coal-mining heritage. Pine Ridge Golf Club has a rolling nine-hole course, and its Pine Ridge Tree-Hugger Two-Person Scramble is scheduled each September.

If fall foliage lured you to take this journey, turn west on Highway 12 and travel the Musselshell River Valley seventy miles from

A room in Reedpoint's restored Montana Hotel Bed and Breakfast
ELIZABETH & WILBUR WOOD PHOTO

Roundup to Harlowton. If you seek longer vistas, however, drive north on Highway 87. Rising through the "breaks" country, you pop out onto a high plain where the Big Snowies suddenly fill the windshield to the northwest. A great dome of limestone, the Snowies surfaced about fifty million years ago, along with other island ranges in this region. Most of the ranges contain more mineral-laden igneous rock than do the Snowies.

At the highest point on this plain, some eight miles north of Roundup, find a good place to pull over and scan the entire horizon. On a clear day you may see the jagged Crazy Mountains a hundred miles to the west and the long Absaroka-Beartooth Front 120 to 180 miles to the southwest, while to the east the plains extend all the way to the Mississippi.

This was the heart of buffalo country. Now it produces cattle, sheep, and wheat. The highway takes you on a roller coaster ride down into stream basins, up onto ridges, down, up, down. Another range of mountains, the Judiths, appears to the north and at Grass-range (where a couple of roadside cafes offer sustenance) Highway 87 turns west into low mountains toward Lewistown and the Judith Basin country.

JUDITH BASIN COUNTRY

Lewistown is a gem whatever time of year you visit, with a number of excellent eating establishments and places to stay, from bed and breakfast to large hotel. Enjoy the shops in the well preserved brick and stone buildings of Main Street. The Whole Famdamily is a fine place to eat, or sample the chili at Poor Man's Books and Coffee. The annual Chokecherry Festival in September features an arts and crafts fair, a 5K run, and lots of street entertainment, including a cherry-pit–spitting contest.

Two nearby lakes are great for camping and boating. Crystal Lake is twenty-four miles west and south of Lewistown (only non-motorized boats are allowed on this small lake in the Snowy Mountains). Or head west toward Hobson on Highway 87, then south onto Montana 400 about seven miles to man-made Ackley Lake (motorized boats and water skiing allowed). Just up the road beyond Hobson is the Meadow Brook Inn Bed & Breakfast (phone 800-318-6423).

At the junction of highways 87 and 191, Eddie's Corner has been open twenty-four hours a day, seven days a week, since 1951. We recommend the tasty Eddie's Burger with its huge plate of fries. Before heading south on Highway 191 toward Judith Gap, check out the long views of five different mountain ranges: the Snowies to the southeast; the Judiths to the east; the Moccasins to the north; the Highwoods in the northwest; and southwest the Little Belt Mountains. You're driving south between the Little Belts and Snowies. Try to cover this territory in daylight—it's well worth it.

South on 191 stop in Garneill at the Ubet Monument, a memorial to early settlers, then moments later drop in at the attractive old Judith Gap Mercantile, composed of three buildings that survived turn-of-the-century fires. The Merc serves good milkshakes and you can browse through a book of old photographs of Judith Gap, Garneill, and Oka.

Farther south comes one of the all-time great Montana views, the dramatic snowclad Crazy Mountains hovering to the southwest, then straight south a longer view to the high peaks of the Absaroka-Beartooth Wilderness.

UPPER MUSSELSHELL

Harlowton, like Lewistown, is self-contained because it's too far to run to Billings. This town has first-run films, a hospital and clinic, and stores offering crafts, secondhand items, antiques, and hardware. An old Milwaukee Railroad electric engine guards Main Street. Near the river are the roundhouse and maintenance yards, and the old depot painted

A hearty welcome awaits visitors
RICK & SUSIE GRAETZ PHOTO

shocking orange. Before the Milwaukee arrived, an earlier line, the Montana Railroad, ran from Lombard, south of Townsend, the Martinsdale—where the splendid Charles M. Bair Family Museum is located (open Wednesdays through Sundays 10 a.m. to 5 p.m. May through September)—then east to Harlowton and north to Lewistown. Reportedly, Helena lawyer Richard Harlow talked so much making deals to finance this railroad that by 1903, when it was completed, it was known as the "Jawbone Railroad."

You can golf in "Harlo" at a nine-hole course with gorgeous views of mountains, camp at Chief Joseph Park, fish at three local reservoirs, or visit the Upper Musselshell Museum (open through Oct. 31 Tuesdays through

Saturdays 10 a.m.- 5 p.m., Sundays 1-4 p.m.) with its full-size replica of the Shawmut dinosaur, Avaceratops, and books on railroad history. The Lammers Ranch near Shawmut has new guest cabins (phone 632-4452), and you can visit the dig where the dinosaur was found.

The Merino Inn opens for breakfast at 6 a.m. and has interesting early photos. The Cornerstone has an excellent beer selection and is open for lunch and dinner. We lament the closing of the Graves Hotel, a favorite pie and coffee stop for travelers, and hope it will open again someday. The classiest Western clothes store in the region is Ray's, at the junction of highways 191 and 12. We never fail to find something elegant.

The Yellowstone River from Sacrifice Cliff, upriver from Billings. Pryor Range on horizon
GARY LEPPART PHOTO

South of Harlowton you'll drive along the east face of the Crazies, with views of the Absaroka and Beartooth ranges as you pass Melville (no gas pumps, but you can pick up lunch and groceries).

Then the route drops back into the Yellowstone Valley, with more autumn yellows and oranges, and crosses the great free-flowing river into Big Timber. This is a weekend that lures you for a return visit, maybe next spring when the cottonwoods are that gorgeous lime green... ✧

Slopes, Sights, & Serenity

by Aaron Kampfe

ALL TOURIST TOWNS HAVE SEASONS; TOWNSPEOPLE SWITCH IN AND OUT OF GEARS AS THE WEATHER changes. Summers in Red Lodge find Broadway lined with motorhomes going to and from Yellowstone National Park. Events fill the summer roster: the Red Lodge Music Festival, the Fourth of July parades and rodeo, the Mountain Man Rendezvous, and the Festival of Nations. But during this "shoulder" season between summer and winter, locals meander down the street and sip lattes in the coffee houses. No hurries. No worries. In early November, traffic on Red Lodge's main street is sparse. Parking is ample. The two-story brick storefronts may or may not have "open" signs. Wander into one of these shops and the sales clerks will chat with you, unconcerned about making a sale. Besides hunting supplies, little is sold in Red Lodge in November. Commerce slows and the locals enjoy the respite. You may enjoy the pace too.

RED LODGE

Red Lodge established a post office in 1884. By the turn of the century, coal mining was its major industry. Immigrants from Europe came to work in the mines; neighborhoods such as Finntown and Little Italy reflect the ethnic groups that settled here.

At Red Lodge Office Supply, pick up a copy of Beverly Rue Wellington's *Red Lodge Landmarks*. This book gives the history of fifty-two structures in Red Lodge. Illustrations are by local artists. The sites include stately Victorian homes in the Highbug district, rural Scandinavian churches, a Finnish boarding house and sauna, and a downtown brothel.

Aspen grove near Red Lodge
GEORGE ROBBINS PHOTO

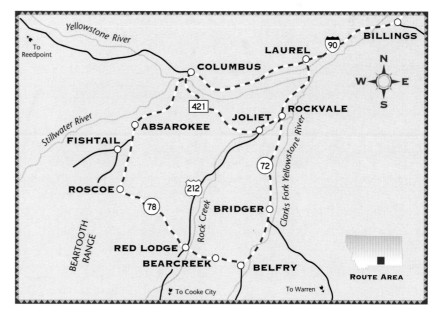

A walking tour of Red Lodge should include a stop at the Carbon County Arts Guild, 11 West 8th, across from the library. Located in an old train depot, the gallery features works by regional artists. The paintings of Mike Kosorok, Phyllis Morfit, Elliot Eaton, Joyce Mackay, and Nellie Israel, as well as jewelry, ceramics, photography, and sculpture are regularly on display. November and December feature a members' show and holiday crafts.

Built in 1893, the Pollard Hotel (800-POLLARD) was the finest in the area, boasting steam heat and electric lights. Recently renovated, the hotel maintains its historic charm. A visit to Red Lodge should include sipping a drink in the Pollard's atrium. I like to kick back in front of the fireplace, ensconced in one of the leather chairs.

For lunch, walk one block west of Broadway on 12th. Between Red Lodge Drug and the Post Office is Bridge Creek. The owner, Peter Christ, provides "simple, honest food, done well." From the dinner menu Chris Harper, the chef, recommended the clam chowder and Indian salmon— smoked, not spicy—served with a honey dijon mayonnaise. The chowder was as good as any I've had in Boston and the salmon was perfect. In my opinion, this food is beyond "simple." But no complaints. The other options are eclectic, with attributes of Asian spices, in-house baked bread, and fresh seafood.

For Mexican food, try Bogart's at 11 South Broadway. The decor includes Humphrey Bogart movie posters, billboards from the 1930s and '40s, and mounted elk, deer, and mountain goats. Bogart's has a great beer selection that includes dark ales from Britain, Australian lagers, and local mircrobrews. The enchiladas, burritos, and chimichangas arrive hot and in generous portions. I recommend the chicken and sour cream enchilada.

Situated at 5,555 feet elevation, Red Lodge might get snow as early as September. But those first snows tend to melt away and still leave plenty of weekends for outings. The weather is capricious,

Snowy-day window shopping along Broadway in Red Lodge
M. D. COLEMAN PHOTO

so take snow boots, gloves, hat, and a warm jacket.

If the snow hasn't fallen yet, the Basin Lakes Trail has easy access, a moderate climb, and great views. Take Highway 212 south through Red Lodge toward the ski area, taking a right after the Chateau Rouge Motel. Drive another four miles then take a left on West Fork Road. The trailhead is on the left. On the trail you'll pass cascading waterfalls, remnants of some cabins, and the bright blue Basin Lakes.

If the snow has fallen, the Silver Run cross-country ski trails are on the same road, about five miles from town. There are trails for every ability, rated easy, intermediate, and advanced. You can glide through the trees or head into the backcountry for some telemarking on the open hillsides.

By November, the high mountains retain the snow and the downhill ski area opens around Thanksgiving. In 1996, Red Lodge Mountain underwent a massive expansion, doubling the size of its terrain. Two new high-speed quad lifts in the Cole Creek drainage added access to seventeen new trails. In 1997, the area continued expanding the snow-making, guaranteeing skiing by the third week in November.

Red Lodge Mountain is one of Carbon County's largest employers, so when it opens the locals switch gears again. Out-of-town cars once again fill Broadway. Parking is not so ample.

ALONG THE BEARTOOTH FRONT

Highway 78 north out of Red Lodge curves up and down hills as it follows the eastern front of the massive Beartooth Range. Around fifty million years ago a great block of the earth's crust was pushed up over 11,000 feet, forming the Beartooths. Slabs of Madison limestone crop out along the front, and you can see the ski runs carved into Grizzly Peak.

Roscoe, along the East Rosebud River, is named after a horse. In 1901, the post office was called Morris, after settler Robert O. Morris. After four years of getting the mail mixed up with Norris, Montana, they changed the name to Roscoe, the name of Mrs. Morris's horse.

In Roscoe, the Grizzly Bar and Restaurant has become a regional attraction. It is not unusual for patrons to drive seventy miles from Billings for the famous prime rib dinners. During the summer, the deck and bar are full of happy eaters and drinkers. At lunchtime in November, however, the atmosphere is strictly local. Ranchers drink coffee at the bar and discuss the price of steers, the fishing, or the elk someone killed. Their brands are painted on the beams: TO Bar, Lazy EL, Top Hat. Many of the local ranching families have been in Roscoe since it was homesteaded around 1900.

Located near Roscoe in the West Rosebud River Valley is a spectacular fishing and hunting camp. J.O. Hash of Black Butte Outfitters (446-3097) offers guided trips on private land. His guests have come from all over the U.S. and Canada, as well as Europe. With white canvas tents, a camp-

fire pit, a mess tent, and horses, the camp resembles an early explorer's camp. But behind the scenes are heated tents, hearty food, and hot showers.

In 1875, the Crow Agency was moved from Mission Creek, near Livingston, to near the present town of Absarokee. In 1882, this portion of the Crow Indian Reservation was opened to settlers and the Indians were once again moved, this time permanently, to Crow Agency south of Billings. A historic marker on Highway 78 explains the transitions.

A mix of vehicles usually lines Absarokee's streets: pickup trucks with bags of minerals for cattle, trailers loaded with logs and heavy machinery headed to and from the Stillwater Mine. Absarokee is a combination agricultural and mining community, and

locals mix in Absarokee's two bars, the Chrome and the Five Spot.

COLUMBUS & JOLIET

Cross the Yellowstone River and you arrive in Columbus. On your left is Montana Silversmiths, a business that employs around 250 people. Since being established in 1973, they've made their belt buckles, hat bands, saddle trim, earrings, and bracelets quintessential Western accessories. Although you can't tour the manufacturing facility, their product is available at Haddy's Shack at 428 E. Pike Ave. and Bruursema Jewelers at 522 Pike Ave.

Red Lodge Mountain guarantees skiing by the third week of November
RICK AND SUSIE GRAETZ PHOTO

With the new development at the Interstate 90 interchange, most who come through Columbus stop at the chain stores and unfortunately miss the downtown and its history. The town began in 1875 as a stage station known as Stillwater; in 1882 the Northern Pacific Railroad built a railroad station. Incorporated in 1907, the town still maintains its early twentieth century flavor. Take some time to stroll Pike Avenue, the main street. The two-story brick buildings still have mom and pop businesses: bookstores, jewelers, drug stores, pizza parlors, and, of course, saloons.

An alternative route to Billings stays off the interstate. Take 416 south of Columbus. You'll pass Itch-Kep-Pe Park, a nice spot to walk along the Yellowstone River. The road to Joliet is mostly paved, with a few miles of gravel. Along the way you'll pass ranches and farms built on the plateaus, with views of the mountains.

In Joliet, stop by the Ringer Gallery on the north side of town. Charles Ringer's recent work includes moving-metal sculptures. Ringer generally works with metals, but mixes some with stained glass and chrome. His kinetic sculptures create the effect of cowboys riding across the range, fish swimming in streams, and buffalo roaming the plains.

BILLINGS

Established in 1882 by the Northern Pacific Railroad, Billings was named for company president Frederick Billings. With rail lines in all directions, two interstate highways, and an international airport, Billings is the hub of oil, agriculture, finance, shopping, and culture in the Northern Rockies.

At the turn of the century the wealthy Preston B. Moss built an elegant home at 914 Division Street. The family lived there until 1984. The mansion, now a museum with original furnish-

ings, ornate ceiling patterns, and woodwork, is open to the public. Hours change seasonally. Call 256-5100 for times.

In 1987 the Fox Theater underwent a $5.3 million renovation and became the Alberta Bair Theater (256-6052). Ann Miller, director of the theater, says, "The Alberta Bair offers a great variety from symphony concerts and ballet to children's shows and jazz. The performing arts center is by no means elitist or one bit snobby. There is something for everyone."

For dining off the beaten path, Na-Ra Restaurant serves Japanese and Korean fare. While you won't find authentic sushi, Na-Ra serves traditional Japanese cuisine: miso soup, green tea, and tempura. On

Sparkle for the crowd at Helena's Festival of Trees
RICK & SUSIE GRAETZ PHOTO

BET ON THE BEARCREEK SALOON'S PIG RACES AND BENEFIT A LOCAL SCHOLARSHIP FUND

the Korean side try the kim chee, a fiery pickled cabbage mixed with pork.

Lodging near downtown is plentiful. Themes range from cowboy western at the Dude Rancher Motel (259-5561), to Victorian elegance at Josephine's B&B (248-5898), to urban convenience at the Radisson Northern Hotel (245-5121).

BRIDGER

From Billings, take I-90 west fourteen miles to Laurel, then head south on Highway 310. As you drive the thirty miles to Bridger, you will notice the fifty-million-year-old Pryor Mountains to the southeast. The exposed rock is mostly Madison limestone, except where streams have cut their canyons into older rocks beneath.

Bridger is named for mountain man Jim Bridger. In 1864, he guided a wagon train bound for Virginia City. He made a ford across the Clarks Fork Yellowstone River, called Bridger Crossing. The third weekend in July, the community celebrates their trapper and explorer heritage with Jim Bridger Days.

The Clarks Fork and Yellowstone river valleys were popular hunting grounds for the Bannock and Nez Perce Indian tribes because herds of buffalo roamed the area. The Mountain Crow

(Absaroka) tribe has traditionally occupied the area, and held vision quests in the Pryor Mountains that rise to the east.

This valley is rich agricultural land, irrigated by the Clarks Fork. Crops include wheat, soy beans, barley, sugar beets, and corn, and the scene has lovely pastoral feel. In November, however, harvest is complete. Fallow fields are plowed in straight rows, red barns dot the landscape, cottonwood tree trunks are silhouetted along the creeks, and the Pryor Mountains dusted with snow rise in the background. Few tourists travel Highway 310 between Billings and the Wyoming towns of Lovell and Cody. Occasionally, bird and game hunters stop through, but mostly the town is quiet and you'll have a relaxing visit.

If you take a left (east) in the center of town and drive eleven miles, you'll find a state fish hatchery open year-round. The Bluewater Spring Trout Hatchery features mostly rainbow trout, but has graylings and cutthroats at times.

On the south end of the main street is a pink building: the Stringtown restaurant, saloon, and casino. The personality of the redheaded proprietor is reflected in her establishment. The motto on her business card reads "A shady place for sunny people (or is it the other way around?)." Inside, the tablecloths have tropical fish patterns, stuffed trout hang on the walls, nets with plastic fish hang over tables, and a fish mobile hangs over the bar. Jungle Jayne, the owner, explained, "I wanted the inside to feel sunny and bright." I recommend Stringtown for those with a sense of humor. The food has a favorable reputation, especially the steak specials: London broil, prime rib, filet with red wine peppercorn sauce. Pizzas, soups, salads, burgers, and sand-

wiches fill out the menu, and your stomach. Even in November, reservations are recommended for weekend dinners (622-3494).

BEARCREEK

Bearcreek began as a coal mining town around 1900 and the first rail load of coal was shipped in September 1906. At its height during World War I, Bearcreek's population reached nearly 2,000. There were mercantiles, hotels, billiard halls, and saloons—but never a church.

As the coal mining industry faded, so did Bearcreek. Abandoned mine shafts, piles of slag, and remnants of old buildings are visible on the landscape. Today Bearcreek is the smallest incorporated city in Montana.

Recently Bearcreek has experienced a slight revival, not from coal mining, but from pigs. Not for slaughter, but for racing. Behind the Bearcreek Saloon lies Bearcreek Downs. The owner makes his money from serving drinks and Mexican food, and donates all the profits from pig racing to a scholarship fund for local students.

A historic marker on the highway just west of town notes the site of the worst mine disaster in Montana history. In February 1943, the Smith Mine collapsed and killed 74 miners. Trapped in the mine and about to face certain death, two miners wrote, "Walter & Johnny. Good-bye wives and daughters. We died an easy death. Love from us both. Be good."

Over the hill from Bearcreek, the route provides a pretty view of the Beartooths before dropping into Red Lodge. If it's early in November, it's still "in-between," still quiet, before the next season begins. But around Thanksgiving or later, you can gear up for a rollicking good time on the slopes. ✧

WINTER

Capitol, Continental Divide, & Cross-Country Skiing

by Bill Hanson

A SPECIAL ATMOSPHERIC CHANGE HITS HELENA AT THE START OF EVERY ODD-NUMBERED YEAR—A FAST-MOVING storm of heat and light created by the Montana Legislature. School kids and special-interest groups come by busloads and caravans to watch and participate in Montana's single largest civics lesson: copper-domed democracy in action.

Four months of legislative action is intense, even feverish; temper-fraying and mind-numbing. Blood pressure testing is a routine capitol event when the Legislature's in session.

But relief and change of pace are an easy weekend drive from Helena. Beautiful, relaxing, mountain-country vistas and interesting small towns stretch along a 200-mile route west over MacDonald Pass to Avon, north to Lincoln and over Flesher Pass back to Helena. Good roads lead to winter pleasures both quiet and boisterous: skiing, snowmobiling, dogsled racing, historic sites, landscapes, and good eats.

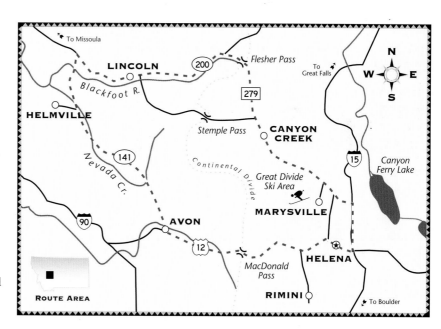

FACING PAGE: *Statue of Thomas Francis Meagher, Montana State Capitol* GINGER DEWIT PHOTO

PRECEDING PAGE: *A homesteader's cabin on Green Mountain, near Noxon* JAY SIMONS PHOTO

ACTION-PACKED VIEWING

Jump-start your Helena adventure with fresh-baked breakfast goodies from one of several downtown bakeries: Park Avenue, Sweetgrass, The Goodie Shop, or The Bagel Company.

Next, find the nerve center of state government power—the Capitol—a kind of over-achieving county courthouse. Montana's Capitol is a neo-classical design, called by some a "temple of democracy" but, to me, it's a good, gray, old lady of a building. It commands a ten-acre slope on the upper east side of town. Repair work is in

The Last Chance Gulch walking mall in Helena
JOHN REDDY PHOTO

progress on the exterior so visitors may find normal foot traffic re-routed.

The gathering of Montana's 150 lawmakers, called simply "the session," might be the state's most closely watched indoor winter sport. Visitors can get help finding the day's action at an information desk on the third floor in the vicinity of the House and Senate chambers. Pamphlets and other handouts guide you through the building, help you find committee hearings, and describe bills under consideration. Daily floor sessions of the Senate and House of Representatives can be viewed from galleries on the fourth floor. But the real work is done by committees that meet in cramped rooms throughout the third and fourth floors where spectators' seating is on a first-come, first-served basis.

Don't leave the Capitol without seeing the art, particularly the Charlie Russell masterpiece mounted on the front wall of the House of Representatives chamber. Paintings by E.S. Paxson are in the House of Representatives lobby. Prized landscapes by Ralph DeCamp are high on the walls of a committee room in the east wing of the third floor. Don't forget to tip your head back for a view of the stained glass ceiling of the rotunda.

The Montana Historical Society Museum is just across the street from the Capitol. C.M. Russell art and memorabilia along with other exhibits of artifacts bring the state's history, prehistory, and culture up close and personal.

Jorgenson's is a comfortable eating place a few blocks north and east of the Capitol on Eleventh Avenue. Fast-food eateries and casino restaurants also abound nearby. Helena's best and brightest often head to Hap's Beer Parlor on Railroad Avenue at the end of a grueling day—or sooner.

TOURING THE TOWN

If logic and common sense are perceived to be rarely applied in legislative action, they are equally rare in Helena's street patterns. The city's first buildings in the 1860s were built along the banks of a meandering creek and some of today's street layout is a legacy of those meanders in Last Chance Gulch—most often called, simply, the gulch. It's Helena's main street downtown.

The Last Chance Gulch walking mall, one of a kind in Montana, has trees growing and people strolling where gold-miners once shoveled and panned. Shops, bars, restaurants, and offices proliferate in new and restored buildings. Gold was first discovered near the restored Colwell Building at the south end of the walking mall, although a plaque on the Montana Club building farther north claims that it's the spot. The south end of the mall is across Park Avenue from the Pioneer Cabin built in 1864. The cabin, preserved as a museum, marks the entrance to Reeder's Alley, a row of shops in restored, quaint brick buildings that once housed bachelor miners. The Stonehouse Restaurant at the end of Reeder's Alley serves fine fare. Nearly everyone's list of favorite eateries on the mall includes The Parrot, renowned for its hand-made candies and old-fashioned soda fountain. Eating places downtown can satisfy most tastes: Yat Son, On Broadway, Rose's Cantina, and Toi's Thai offer ethnic variety. The Windbag Saloon & Grill and the Rialto Bar and Grill have loyal customers. Bert & Ernie's has terrific gourmet pizzas. Coney Island is a great place for uncommonly good lunchtime hot dogs and their wall murals are very entertaining.

Mount Helena, a 700-acre city park, dominates the western horizon. Several trails lead around the lower slopes or up to the mountain's 5,468-foot peak. Since Helena lies in a semi-arid region, chances are good in many winters that no snow blocks the trails.

Helena has a riot of architectural types that are unexpected in a Western town. The gems are noted on maps available from the Helena Chamber of Commerce Visitor's Center, corner of Sixth and Cruse avenues. The must-see list includes mansions on both the east and west sides of town; the state's original governor's mansion; the Myrna Loy Center for the Performing Arts, formerly a jail; the Cathedral of St. Helena; the Holter Museum of Art; the red-tile–roofed buildings of Carroll College; and the Helena Civic Center's mosque-style architecture complete with minaret.

GETTING AWAY

Westbound from Helena, you can be atop 6,325-foot MacDonald Pass in less than half an hour, but that means missing several attractions just outside Helena. The Archie Bray Foundation, on Country Club Avenue, is renowned among potters and ceramics collectors. You can stop by the gallery store or wander back into the studios to talk to the artists.

Just as Highway 12 begins to climb the pass, turn south on Tenmile Road toward the once-thriving mining community of Rimini and "Helena's backyard wildlands." There are numerous trails for cross-country skiing and snowmobiling off this road.

U.S. Highway 12 over the Continental Divide is heavily used, but expansion to four lanes nudged it out of the white-knuckle category. Frontier Town, near the top, is a favorite of cross-country skiers for its seventeen miles of groomed trails.

Weather? If you don't like it, wait a minute, it'll change. That's not so much of a cliché on this weekend route because you'll criss-cross and travel along the edges of three National Weather Service forecast zones. About half the route lies on the edge of one zone that the Weather Service says has the mildest winter temperatures in the state. But our route takes us close to Rogers Pass, too, where the lowest official temperature in the continental United States, -70°F., was recorded January 20, 1954. And, we're skirting the edge of still another zone that has been described as the battleground of Arctic and Pacific air masses.

You can get more than the menu's "incredi-bull food" at the Avon Family Cafe: a wood-burning stove smack-dab in the middle of the cozy place makes a mid-winter visit particularly worthwhile.

Turn onto Montana Route 141

at Avon, and drive north through a beautiful valley with mountains on all horizons—the Garnet Range to the west, the Scapegoat Mountains to the north, and the Continental Divide to the east. Gold miners worked this area in the late 1800s, leaving behind the ghost town of Blackfoot City northeast of Avon.

Route 141 through the Nevada Creek Valley has light traffic and no billboards. Nevada Creek flows into a reservoir of the same name that looks good for fishing, but isn't. At the southeast end of the reservoir, the Fitzpatrick Ranch, listed on the National Register of Historic Places, is worth a closer look. Composed of nine buildings, some log, the ranch was built in the 1870s.

Helmville, about a mile off the highway, has enough activity to keep the Copper Queen Saloon going, as well as two churches, a school, post office, and a handful of homes. Ghostly buildings are scattered through town, wonderfully weathered wood shells burnished and dappled brown and gold.

Route 141 ends as it crosses the

Frontier Town, atop MacDonald Pass
RICK GRAETZ PHOTO

Blackfoot River and meets Highway 200. Here, the higher-elevation landscape is rock and scree fields with lodgepole pine, whitebark pine, subalpine fir, and a few alpine meadows. Spruce survive along some stream bottoms where forests of subalpine fir, Douglas-fir, and ponderosa pine once proliferated. Now there are stretches of fescue grasslands with pines that have been deformed by punishing winds.

The Blackfoot, revered among fisherfolk and others, has become a lightning rod of controversy over a proposed, large, open-pit gold mine east of Lincoln, practically within spitting distance of the headwaters of the Blackfoot. Many worry that the proposed mine's cyanide leaching process to extract gold from ore spells doom for the Blackfoot. This is not just any old river: the Blackfoot inspired Norman Maclean's *A River Runs Through It*.

LINCOLN

Highway 200 today is an easy, comfortable route through the Blackfoot Canyon into Lincoln. Most traffic just passes through, including Meriwether Lewis who was the first tourist in the area to record his party's overnight stay on July 6, 1806. Lewis camped at the mouth of what later was named Lincoln Gulch.

Other visitors of note: Charlie Russell, who vacationed frequently in Lincoln in the early decades of this century; and Sam McGee, immortalized in the Robert Service poem, "The Cremation of Sam McGee," who reportedly spent the winter of 1934 in Lincoln. That report comes from the Upper Blackfoot Valley Historical Society's captivating book, *Gold Pans and Singletrees*. There's also the report of a Helena prostitute who arrived as a summer visitor and stayed on for the winter. When streams froze and cut off the cash flow of local prospectors, the enterprising woman opened a number of "charge accounts" for her customers. The woman's house caught fire one night and some miners were among the volunteer firefighters. The book of charge accounts was missing after the fire.

Lincoln's economy today depends a lot on stockgrowers, loggers, and traffic on U.S. 200, along with an increasing seasonal influx of recreationists, especially summer-home owners, hunters, guides and outfitters, cross-country skiers, snowmobilers, and dogsledders. An early 20th-century rodeo bronc rider, Fanny Sperry Steele, among the first women inducted into the

Willow-lined tributary of the Blackfoot River near Lincoln
GEORGE WUERTHNER PHOTO

National Cowboy Hall of Fame, once operated a ranch and outfitting service with her husband west of Lincoln.

Lincoln has an industrial success story in Hi-Country Beef Jerky. Its plant and adjacent store are about three miles west of town. On a smaller scale, Rick Rowley is a one-man factory in town, where he turns out rough-hewn wood sculptures. The works are on display and for sale at Lost Woodsman Gallery, which also has a cafe offering intriguing, generous sandwiches and espresso.

Highway 200 through town is a business strip and more. Motels, service stations, stores, bars, and restaurants crowd along its length, jostling for space with a bank, arts and crafts shops, churches, a school, and a park. Garland's Town & Country store has outdoor garb and equipment and souvenirs. The Lincoln Lodge, a grand old two-story log structure listed on the National Register of Historic Places, has eighteen rustic but comfortable rooms (bathrooms down the hall) and a restaurant. The 7-Up Ranch Supper Club a few miles east of town maintains a reputation for good food.

When talk here turns to 7-Up, by the way, it's not about a clear, carbonated soft drink. "Seven Up Pete" was a kind of poker game in the mid-1800s when prospector Iver Wulff arrived in an area east of Lincoln. According to *Gold Pans and Singletrees*, Wulff was so good at the game he was nicknamed 7-Up Pete. The area he successfully prospected became 7-Up Pete Gulch. Today, the Seven-Up Pete Joint Venture is a Lincoln-based project of Canyon Resources, which is planning the controversial open pit gold mine called the McDonald Gold Project.

Lincoln residents know how to live it up in winter, especially as word spreads of exceptional snowmobile conditions. Cabin Fever Days are in mid-February and include events such as snowboot volleyball and kickball. Several weekends in January and February have a snowmobile-related event scheduled in town or on the more than 200 miles of groomed trails nearby. One good source of information is April Woodhouse at Summit Seekers Sales and Rentals, 362-4078.

COMPLETING THE LOOP

A turnoff ten miles east of Lincoln puts you on the Flesher Pass road, County Road 279, southeast toward Helena. The road, recently resurfaced and well-maintained, climbs through several switchbacks to 6,131-foot Flesher Pass, your second crossing of the Continental Divide. An alternative is the graveled Stemple Pass Road that starts in Lincoln. Stemple Pass Road joins County Road 279 twenty-three miles south of Lincoln. Both Stemple and Flesher passes are popular with cross country skiers.

You might want to take a break at the Canyon Creek Store, about twenty miles from Helena. The store also serves as the Canyon Creek Post Office and has a rare, rural small-town flavor. The store celebrated its 125th birthday in 1996.

Watch for the turnoff to Marysville, a partial ghost town that once had a population of 4,000 and still gets lively at a popular eating place, the Marysville House. Great Divide Ski Area is just up the hill from Marysville, offering downhill skiing and some of the least expensive lift tickets in the state. Owner Kevin Taylor summed it up: "We're cheap and we're local." Cross-country skiing also is available in the area.

Back on Highway 200, the road goes through prairie-like landscape. There you'll find Montana Al's Silver City Bar. Owner Al Potter maintains what is likely the world's largest collection of Fender guitars, but displays only about one fourth of it. ✧

Paradise, Predators, & Play in the Park

by Lynette Dodson

WHILE I WAS GROWING UP IN LIVINGSTON DURING THE MID-'70S, ONE OF THE BEST THINGS A FRIEND of mine and I found to do on winter weekends was drive to Cooke City. Striking out on a Sunday afternoon, we'd fill up the gas tank, grab snacks, and head off into another world. Silent and snow covered. Populated mostly by the hoofed, winged, antlered, and furry set. Roads, though plowed, were intermittently scary. Add the thrill of sneaking out of state (the route dips in and out of nearby Wyoming) but ending up in the same county we had started in.

"Where've you been?" my parents would ask when we'd finally return home.

"Nowhere."

That was then. But even now it still can be said that there is nowhere else better to be any time of the year.

LIVINGSTON

The logical beginning for this 110-mile point-to-point route is Livingston. Say you're fresh off the interstate. Maybe you're hauling a trailer with snowmobiles, or have cross country skis strapped to the top of your vehicle. You might arrive with snowshoes or ice skates in the trunk. Quite possibly you've come with your camera, laptop, or journal. Or

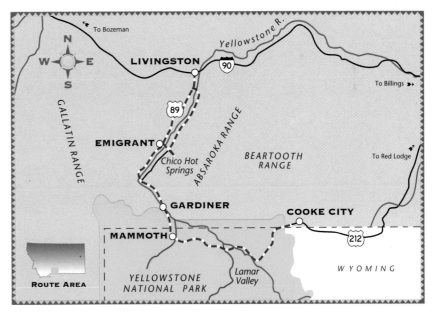

simply with a good book to finish or a sketch to work on. Artists of any medium will be in good company, for you're likely to rub elbows with some of the plethora of painters, photographers, and writers who have chosen to inhabit the area.

Nestled at the base of the Absaroka Mountains, Livingston has a lot of personality (and personalities) in the winter months. The four-story Murray Hotel across from the renovated Depot Center is the cornerstone of Livingston's historic downtown

Winter solitude in the Beartooth Range
RICK GRAETZ PHOTO

district. If you're looking for other accommodations, check with The Innskeeper. I'm intrigued by a rental called The Centennial, a railroad mail car renovated in "turn of the century elegance," located just four miles south of town on the banks of the Yellowstone River. Love old stone houses with hardwood floors? The Greystone Inn Bed and Breakfast is within walking distance from downtown Livingston. The Innskeeper can also find you a cozy mountain cabin at the base of Livingston Peak, or an entire house to rent. Call 222-5456 or 800-590-5456.

Railroad-birthed in 1882, Livingston in the late 1990s is an eclectic mix of Old West and new. Amble down Park Street past the steamy windows of the Livingston Leaf and Bean. In the New West, coffee shops rival saloons as the social hub.

I send my women friends to The Obsidian Collection for fashionable clothing. Bookworms can spend hours browsing through the O'Byrnes' extensive and affordable selection of rare and used books. Timber Trails Outdoor Company is "user friendly" and offers winter outdoor recreation information along with equipment rentals and sales.

Some things don't change. Gil's Gift Shop still's "got it." Sax and Fryer has sold books, stationery, and art supplies since 1883. At the Mint Bar, you can examine amazing images of trains while nursing a shot of Bailey's Irish Cream.

These days we joke that in Livingston "you can eat your way around the world." Uncle Looie's

Paradise Valley and the Yellowstone River
CAROL POLICH PHOTO

Subzero morning in Livingston
PAUL DIX PHOTO

on Park Street presents "The Finest in Italian Dining." Got a craving for Chinese food? Step next door to The Wok. The newly renovated Livingston Bar and Grille offers fine continental dining, while the Sport provides American-style steaks, chicken, and ribs amidst walls decorated with articles of bygone years. Both the Beartooth Diner and The Crazy Coyote serve authentic Mexican fare.

November is the quietest time. Come then if you want to read or write, or hunt in the mountains (not so quiet). During the holiday season, you'll not lack for things to do. On December's first weekend, Santa comes to town on top of a firetruck for "Christmas in Paradise," and there are hayrides, caroling, and the "Lighting of the Lights" on the gigantic Children's Tree. The third weekend is Livingston's biggest dress-up affair, the Christmas Ball, featuring live jazz. The popular Firehouse 5 Theater presents a special Christmas show each year. Check the Danforth, Wade, and Visions West galleries for special holiday exhibits.

THE PARADISE

Leave for "Cooke" when you've had your fill of Livingston. Call (406) 222-3831 to find out what you can expect road- and weather-wise. Fill your gas tank. Pack blankets and snacks and a swimsuit before you stop by the local Forest Service office on the way out of town, for maps and information detailing outdoor recreation.

The Yellowstone River cuts south from its Yellowstone National Park origins, creating a valley blessed even yet with wonderful vistas, fresh flowing water, and abundant wildlife. The valley's name is attributed to a pioneer daughter who, upon viewing her new Montana home, is said to have exclaimed "It's just like paradise." The Absaroka Mountains to the east and the Gallatins to the west are composed of rock spewed from repeated volcanic eruptions, uplifted and weathered over the last fifty million years.

Take the Mill Creek turnoff to the East River Road. Drive ten more miles east to a parking lot near Snowbank Campground. Here both ski and snowmobile trails are marked, but not all are groomed. Beginning skiers can try out the mile-long Snowbank Campground loop. If you're more ambitious try the ten-mile round trip Passage Creek Trail, a forested route that takes you by old homesteads and ends at Passage Falls.

Snowmobilers might like to head straight east alongside Mill Creek. Sledding for old and young alike is also a possibility in this area. Check with an Avalanche Control Center at 587-6981 before setting out in any backcountry area.

Midway through the valley, Chico Hot Springs resort can be found four miles east of the river. Here awaits a steaming ninety-eight-degree natural hot springs pool. You can also make arrangements for dogsled treks, hayrides, cross-country skiing, and a relaxing professional massage. The Chico Inn dining is renowned.

Ice fishing on your mind? The turnoff for Dailey Lake, stocked with trout and walleye, is marked four miles south of Chico.

GARDINER

Highway 89 climbs through an increasingly interesting geologic landscape that includes the high and narrow metamorphic walls

**FOR THE TRIP
TOWARD COOKE
CITY, PACK SWIM
SUITS ALONG WITH
WINTER GEAR**

of Yankee Jim Canyon and the exposed red sandstone of the Devil's Slide. Decked with a dusting of snow, the slide is a sight to behold.

Gardiner moves at a slow waltz in winter, and lodgings are easy to come by. Helen, of Helen's Corral Drive-In, can be bound flipping her famous Hateful Hamburgers for the late elk hunting crowd. The K-Bar serves a good homemade pizza and the Two-Bit Saloon serves breakfast and a complimentary cup of coffee for the 7 to 10 a.m. crew. In late December, drop by the Blue Goose Saloon for a glass of holiday cheer.

YELLOWSTONE IN WINTER

You can't miss driving through historic Roosevelt Arch as you enter Yellowstone, the nation's—and world's—first national park. A hotbed of past and present volcanic activity, Yellowstone is the largest active caldera in the world. At the 45th parallel—exactly halfway between the equator and the North Pole—a steaming bank indicates a great place to swim in the Gardiner

IT'S NOT UNUSUAL TO HAVE A "BISON JAM" STOPPING TRAFFIC, SINCE THE WARMER BLACK ROAD SURFACE ATTRACTS THE ANIMALS IN THE WINTER

River. Soaking in the hot waters that cascade off the cliffs at "Boiling River" is a wonderful experience, but be aware of the river's swift-moving icy water and slippery cliffs. It takes a determined person to walk through the snow and then put on a bathing suit, but it's worth it.

Mammoth Hot Springs was formerly known as Fort Yellowstone. I love the red clay tile roofs and elegant architecture of the buildings. Check out the carved stone bears in front of one office building. Most park services shut down about mid-October each year, except for the Visitor Center. You won't find the Mammoth Hot Springs Hotel and Restaurant open until late December, but the local, privately owned Hamilton Store sets up tables and serves soup and sandwiches throughout November and December.

The Horace M. Albright Visitor Center, named for the first National Park Service superintendent of Yellowstone, contains must-know information for park travelers in all seasons. The nearby Mammoth Terraces are composed of limestone and calcium carbonate combined with heat, water and carbon dioxide. The delicate and beautiful terraces are surrounded by one-and-a-half miles of boardwalk for easy viewing.

Yellowstone is noted for cross-country skiing amidst landscape and wildlife. Skiers can combine sightseeing and sporting fun by taking the one-and-a-half-mile Upper Terrace Loop that begins at the Upper Terrace parking lot. If you feel like a real workout, go almost a half-mile south of the Upper Terrace parking lot and find Snow Pass trail, which loops four miles back to a snow vehicle trail.

Shuttle service for skiers is available to Tower Junction and Blacktail Plateau, other favorite ski trails on the route to Cooke City.

NINE MONTHS OF WINTER

The route to Cooke City is the only road in the park kept open during the winter months. Don't be in a hurry: it's narrow, potholed, and can be icy. It's not unusual to have a "bison jam" stopping traffic, since the warmer black road surface attracts the animals in the winter.

Highway 212 crosses glacial till, moraines, boulders, and other leftover evidence of Ice Age activity. The road eventually meets up with the Lamar River and passes through its namesake valley. At other times of the year, black bear and even grizzlies can be spotted on the fossil- and petrified tree-lined ridges of the Lamar Valley. In winter there is a plenitude of the larger herbivores, including bison and elk who feed in the valley's sheltered climate. Here too are coyotes who feed on deceased members of the herds. If you are extremely lucky, perhaps you may spot even a wolf!

It is surprising to realize that upon arriving in Cooke City (population 90) you are back in Park County. The heavily timbered high country here at almost 7,700 feet elevation differs remarkably from the lower elevation starting point in Livingston.

Mount Republic, the visible point for a major thrust fault, stands guard over this area. Here, intense geologic activity captured many ore and mineral deposits that are coveted even today. When proposed, the New World Mine, located five miles from the city center, sparked controversy across the nation.

Cooke City is known as the land of "nine months of winter." Snow starts in October, can pile up over six feet high, and doesn't leave in some places until June or even July. This is a primo outdoor recreation spot.

Snow machines are big in

Gray wolf CANIS LUPUS
M.A. MCDONALD PHOTO

"Cooke." During winter they're the major method of transportation for many residents. Cooke City Exxon will sell you a tank of gas, or, if you didn't bring your own, fix you up with a snowmobile rental for $150 a day. Maps provided by the Cooke City Snowmobile Club are available around town. These trails are jumping off points to the vast expanse of local winter "play areas." Take heed: this is avalanche country, and you must stay out of designated wilderness areas.

Warm Creek Trail is an easy and sheltered three miles into Yellowstone National Park, then back again. Drive back to Silvergate, then hop on the trail at the southwest corner of town. Or strike out east on Highway 212 for a longer ski route: about three-quarters of a mile out of town, you will find Lulu Trail. Snowmobilers also share this route. You can loop back four miles to your starting point or branch off north on Round Lake Trail, which doubles your trip. Warning: Round Lake Trail climbs to over 10,000 feet and passes through storm country.

Though many Cooke City businesses close for winter months, you'll find a great piece of pie at Mountain Treasures gift shop year-round. Next door, the High Country Motel provides clean and comfortable lodging for about $40 a night. A few blocks away, the Miner's Saloon has a full bar, food, and live music on weekend nights. Try the Pine Tree Cafe at the end of town for a good and hearty breakfast.

Remember that Cooke City is, as Mountain Treasures owner Richard Kotar will tell you, "one of the last true frontier towns." At Christmastime in Cooke, do as the locals do: provide your own entertainment.

Back home again, when your eyes get a faraway look of steamy hot pools and empty highways, you'll know what to tell them when they ask where you've been: "Nowhere." ✧

Surprises, Skiing, & Scenery

by Jay Simons

SURPRISE, SURPRISE! THAT'S WHAT AWAITS YOU IN NORTHWESTERN MONTANA IN WINTER. EVERY TURN of the highway, every wrinkle in the mountains, every sunrise and sunset is pure delight when you get out for this 330-mile tour of our wintry land.

Last year, we had twenty feet of snow at Noxon and the only way to get to the barn to feed my horse was to ski there—over my mature fruit trees. That was a bit much, but I have to admit it was a new experience and that's what many of us look for.

NORTHERN FLATHEAD

The people of Whitefish (population 4,500+) have an unabashed enthusiasm for snow. One of the best reasons to visit this town in January and February is the Winter Carnival—cure the winter blahs, strut your stuff, and just plain have fun. The festival is the first weekend of February, but residents start getting in the mood in January when they crown the "royal family."

The carnival starts on The Big Mountain on Friday, when King Ullr raises his sword to bring scores of torch-bearing skiers down the slopes, lit overhead by fireworks. A parade, ice sculpture contest, kiddie carnival, and parade are other carnival highlights. Pie, coffee, and jazz pre-

sented by the Flathead Jazz Society are served up at St. Charles Catholic Church. Street and snow games take place in the field east of Whitefish Depot. Don't miss the downtown art walk. Sunday, Whitefish Rotarians serve "Can't Be Beat" pancakes at the Whitefish Moose Lodge, and there are ski races at the Whitefish Nordic Center west of town.

Ready to shake off the snow and warm your innards? My favorite Whitefish restaurant for lunch is The Kitchen Connection and Two Sisters Antiques. Their robust lentil soup, and thick slice of oatmeal/molasses/ whole wheat bread is hearty fare for a winter

Snowghosts on The Big Mountain
RICK & SUSIE GRAETZ PHOTO

day. Tuck a raspberry scone into your pack to eat later.

Whitefish shops offer unique handmade clothing, jewelry, leathercraft, pottery, and fine arts. The Great Northern Brewing

Flathead Lake's northwest corner
RICK & SUSIE GRAETZ PHOTO

Company downtown has a tasting room. For you beer fans, the Winter Microbrew Festival on The Big Mountain is January 30.

Fresh-brewed coffee is especially welcome in winter. Taste Grizzly Blend or huckleberry coffee at The Montana Coffee Traders located south of the junction of highways 93 and 40.

Kalispell (population 27,697) is situated near the confluence of the Stillwater, Whitefish, and Flathead rivers. The Hockaday Center for the Arts has three galleries of historical and contemporary work. You can cross-country ski the Buffalo Hills Golf Course right on into Lawrence Park. Big Sky Rides provide horse-drawn trolley rides and luxurious carriage tours. Bundle up and go!

Shop 'til you drop at Kalispell Center Mall, in Cavanaugh's or shops that specialize in Montana-inspired gifts and apparel. Then dine in a garden beneath the sixty-foot-skylight in the Atrium Restaurant at the Inn.

WESTERN FLATHEAD

Check out the scenic thirteen-mile frontage on Flathead Lake near Somers and Lakeside for good ice fishing. The Montana Grill specializes in mesquite-grilled fresh fish, and great steaks and prime rib.

Somers once was a mill town owned by the Somers Lumber Company. The Somers Cafe, located in a 1905 bank building, has the original floor, walls, and vault, and displays musical instruments on the walls. Fridays, they serve a thick, wonderful, clam chowder.

A mile down the highway, The Osprey Bed and Breakfast (800-258-2042), is open in the winter by reservation. It's a tranquil place on the banks of the Flathead. Sharon Finney said a stay at her B&B is "like going to your favorite aunt's home. She entertains and waits on you and you don't have to make the bed." Ask if she'll share some of the homemade pickles they put up last summer.

Also in Somers is an antique-lovers' delight, The Osprey Nest Antiques. Owner Karen Nagelhus has a mix of 18th century glassware and furniture, as well as rare and unusual items. The setting has inspired articles in *Architectural Digest* and *Traditional Home*.

Before you hit Highway 28, a turnoff leads to Lake Mary Ronan, a popular ice fishing spot for kokanee salmon, rainbow trout, perch, and bass.

HOT SPRINGS

You'll read about Hot Springs before you ever get there because the town's business people have placed Burma Shave–type signs on fenceposts. There are several places in Hot Springs where you can take mineral-water baths, but many prefer to "go native" up Spring Street, where there are free open-air plunges and mud baths. Park your car, walk to the pool, and slide in. The water is hot. The mud baths are primitive: lower yourself down to the warm mud, and slather it on. It's great! After it dries, you can wash the caked, black stuff off your body with a garden hose—brrr—then run back over to the hot springs and warm up. Bring your own towels.

Hot Springs isn't a fancy town, but it has the essentials. The buffalo burgers with pepper cheese and alfalfa sprouts at Courtner's Cafe are really tasty.

ALONG THE CLARK FORK

It's mountainous between Hot Springs and Plains. For a real down-home, family-oriented weekend, visit Vicki and Gerry

Carr's Cabinet Mountain Guest Ranch (826-3970), off Highway 28. The Carrs provide horse-drawn wagon rides and horseback riding. The llamas they use as pack animals are curious critters, sleeping close to the guest house at night.

The people of Plains are tenacious. Large blocks of business establishments were twice destroyed by fire, but residents have rebuilt them in the style of the original buildings.

Wildlife is abundant along Highway 200. You might spot deer, elk, moose, coyotes, and bighorn sheep. Winter is the best time to see wildlife down low. Eight miles east of Thompson Falls are several areas where more than 500 bighorn sheep come down near the highway to eat in the fields. I've seen as many as one hundred at the KooKooSint Mountain Sheep Viewing Area. Closer to Thompson Falls, they sometimes stand in the highway licking salt from the road. November and December is mating season and you might be lucky enough to see or hear the rams knocking heads, vying for the females.

In 1809, geographer and trapper David Thompson established the Saleesh House trading post, and described what is now named Thompson Falls. The Montana Power Company built a dam in 1916, creating a two-mile-long reservoir that covered the falls. The mighty Clark Fork River may have been tamed some, but there's still plenty of water moving rapidly through the gorges. Ice fishing is really popular and some really big northern pike are taken out of the river. Anglers bring their big fish to Ernie Franke at Krazy Ernie's Emporium on Main Street for official weighing and measuring.

The Blue Spruce Lodge (827-4762) at Trout Creek has a great view of the Clark Fork River valley. The lodge was designed and built by Russ Milleson, who became a quadraplegic following an industrial accident. The lodge is barrier-free and wheelchair accessible. There's snowmobiling and cross-country skiing from the lodge, and guests are treated to gourmet meals.

Four miles east of Noxon, one of Montana's largest earth-filled dams and hydroelectric projects backs up water thirty-seven miles to Thompson Falls. Noxon attracted national attention

The Gemrich boys dousing their dad in the mud baths in Hot Springs
JAY SIMONS PHOTO

because of the Militia of Montana, but there are no camouflage-wearing, armed men walking the streets. It is a quiet little community worth crossing the river to see. The Past, Present & Pawn antique shop owners, Danny and Mary Schacht, refinish and display fine furniture. The Larkin family opened a restaurant in which three generations of women cook and serve good, home-style meals. A local watering spot, Toby's Fabulous Valley Bar, has more than $20,000 in Susan B. Anthony silver dollars embedded in the bar, walls, and ceiling.

THROUGH THE CABINETS

The Bull River Road (Highway 56 west of Noxon) is one of northwest Montana's most scenic drives. It's curvy and you'll share the two-laner with loaded log trucks, so take your time.

The Big Horn Lodge (847-5597) is a combination of southern plantation manor and Montana hunting lodge. Inez Wates' background as an interior decorator, landscape designer, and airline hostess is the perfect combination in this business. Her son, Rus Willis, a big-game outfitter, has provided trophy mounts for the

walls. Cross-country skiers can tour the meadow below the lodge or drive to the trail in Ross Creek Cedars.

I admire the spirit of the people in Libby. When a 1990s windstorm broke off many tall trees, they carved the stumps into interesting images. That kind of character keeps this community alive despite the loss of a thousand jobs in recent years when major employers—two mines and a sawmill—pulled out. It's still a timber town but residents are trying to broaden the economic base.

I like to dine at the Hidden

Chapel on Utah Avenue. Formerly a church, it has been converted into an intimate restaurant. The chicken strudel contains tender, savory pieces of chicken tossed with spinach, onion, muenster cheese, and white wine, folded into a phyllo pastry and baked. Fresh bread is served with huckleberry butter.

The scenic Kootenai Falls are

The low angle of winter sunlight brightens the high peaks in the Cabinet Range
DONALD M. JONES PHOTO

five miles west of Libby. There are plenty of ungroomed forest roads nearby for cross-country skiing and snowmobiling.

KOOCANUSA COUNTRY

The name Koocanusa was coined by the residents of Rexford, whose original townsite was flooded by the reservoir. It's from the words Kootenai, Canada and USA. The Libby Dam Visitor Center isn't open in winter, but you can easily see the dam from the highway. It's quite a piece of engineering. North of Koocanusa Bridge are huge cascades of ice over giant stone buttresses. It's fun to stop and watch the ice climbers.

The weather is relatively mild in Eureka, which calls itself the Christmas Tree Capital of the World; timber and farming form the economic base. The lake below Huckleberry Hannah's Bed & Breakfast south of Eureka is great for ice skating, fishing, and cross-country skiing the perimeters. Innkeepers Jack and Deanna Doying are a kick, and love to run "Mystery Weekends" where groups gather in costume to solve a mystery.

Eureka, population 1,200, has Sophie's Emporium. Owner Barbara Ingram's deli and espresso shop also is a showcase for the arts and crafts of locals. Bunny's Country Kitchen makes the best huckleberry milkshakes I've ever tasted. Just up the block is Brown's Pottery, owned by Robert and Johanna Brown. All their pottery is made on site and browsers can watch the Browns at work. Their shop also carries the work of many local artisans, including silver, woodcarvings, leather, and beadwork.

COMPLETING THE LOOP

The Point of Rocks Restaurant near Olney doesn't look like much

LIBBY HAS ITS OWN CHARACTER. WHEN A WINDSTORM BROKE OFF MANY TALL TREES IN LIBBY, THE PEOPLE CARVED THE STUMPS INTO INTERESTING SHAPES

from the road, but their prime rib and shrimp combo is zesty, with huge, succulent shrimp.

Jeff Ulsamer, of Dog Sled Adventures, located two miles north of Olney, promises that a ride will be the highlight of your winter. Two adults can ride together "like a human burrito," bundled up in elk and deer hides tucked inside a bag that is fastened to the sled. Anxious to go, the dogs yip and jump around in their harnesses. When he releases the brake, suddenly you're off, traveling "at the speed of dog— forty to forty-five paws," he joked, or the equivalent of thirty miles per hour. Once on the trail, it's very quiet. It's a wonderfully exciting, yet peaceful, experience. Reservations are required: call 881-2275.

Many Montanans fly to warmer climes for a winter holiday because they don't know what good times await them right here at home. Not me. There are too many people and too much traffic down south. Better a getaway in northwestern Montana, where cold weather brings beautiful vistas and beckoning ski trails.

See you on the road. ✧

Museums, Moguls, & Missouri River

by Beverly R. Magley

DON'T LET WINTER KEEP YOU FROM WEEKEND TRAVEL. HIGHWAY CREWS KEEP THE ROADS CLEAR AND sanded on this 325-mile route, and getting out and about is sure to prevent the midwinter blues. Additionally, holiday celebrations and decorations provide extra reasons to travel this loop in November and December.

HELENA

Beginning in Helena, fortify yourself with a down-home breakfast at the No Sweat Cafe on Last Chance Gulch (don't be in a rush—regulars joke that the cafe boasts same-day service). Walk a block to the Holter Museum of Art to view the art display and perhaps pick up one-of-a-kind holiday gifts at their Winter Showcase, mid-November to December 31. This annual exhibition and sale of regional arts and crafts provides a rich variety of styles from 100 artists in the Northwest region, in media including ceramics, jewelry, handwoven clothing, paintings, and prints.

One block up the hill is the Cathedral of St. Helena. This gothic edifice, finished in 1914, was financed primarily by Thomas

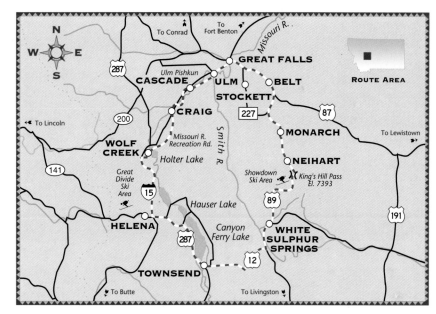

Ready to run at Showdown
RICK AND SUSIE GRAETZ PHOTO

Cruse, who made his fortune in gold taken from nearby Marysville's Drumlummon Mine. The cathedral's north entrance is generally open during the day, and sun streaming through the stained-glass windows illuminates the impressive interior and marble statues.

Downtown Helena's annual

Winter Art Walk is in mid-November. Over 20 businesses feature an array of fine arts, ceramics, beadwork, and more. You can ride a horsedrawn carriage between the more than 1,000 luminarias that light the way.

Helena is known as a family town, and children find much to entertain them. On Saturday after

Thanksgiving, children can have a free Breakfast with Santa at the Stonehouse Restaurant in Reeder's Alley. Pep up their spirits every Saturday afternoon between Thanksgiving and Christmas with storytelling at the library. If you're lucky enough to be in Helena the first weekend of December, check out the fairyland Festival of Trees at the Civic Center—the decorated trees are an inspiration, live entertainment varies from senior tap-dancers to high school choral groups, and the proceeds benefit Intermountain Children's Home.

Set aside several hours to see the capital complex. Volunteers guide tours of the Montana State Capitol, which houses magnificent paintings by C.M. Russell, impressive stained-glass windows, and the historic rotunda. Across the street, the Montana Historical Society Museum's permanent displays are interesting and informative. Their special exhibits hall features changing theme-shows.

The wildlife display in the lobby of Fish, Wildlife & Parks on Sixth Avenue includes fish, a mountain goat, moose, bison, grizzly bear, various waterfowl, and a bald eagle.

The Archie Bray Foundation on Country Club Avenue provides ceramicists a unique opportunity to work on their craft in the historic brickyard complex. The grounds are open year-round, and it's a delight to walk around and discover the many pieces of art exhibited outdoors. Some are secreted under vegetation or nestled in snowbanks, others are extravagantly displayed. All are interesting. The sales gallery is open Monday through Saturday, 10 a.m. to 5 p.m. and Sundays 1 to 5 p.m.

Had enough looking and ready for some action? The Broadwater Athletic Club's Adventure Zone costs $4.95 for two hours of play for children ages 5-13. It offers an assortment of fun equipment: balls and slides and trolley bars, net climbs, rope climbs, an air hop, a deep ball-bin, and a monkey maze. Parents can soak in the outdoor hot-springs pool while their kids run off a lot of energy.

Locals head for skating rinks scattered around town, or skate indoors at the Queen City Ice Palace. If the weather has cooperated—i.e., clear, calm, and cold for a long time—Spring Meadow State Park has acres of smooth ice and a knockout view of Mount Helena City Park. Stay away from the west end, where springs make the ice unsafe in even the coldest winter.

Great Divide is Helena's local downhill ski area. This small, family-oriented enterprise has surprisingly good runs, and improvements are made every

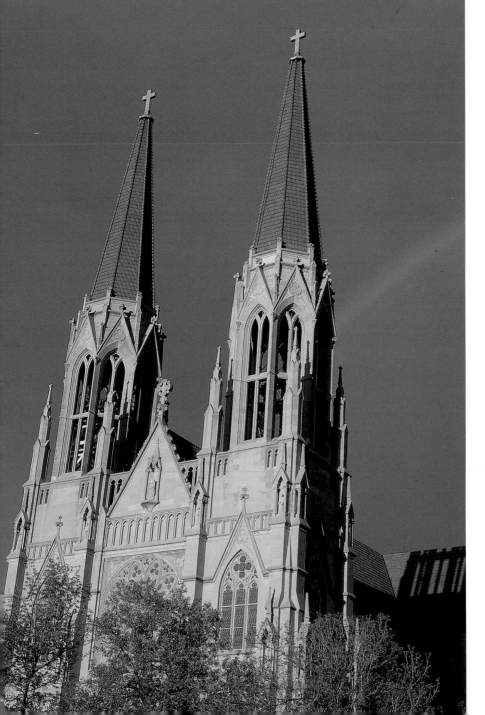

Cathedral of St. Helena
JOHN LAMBING PHOTO

year. About 60 trails cover three different drainages. Great Divide usually opens Thanksgiving weekend, and full-day lift tickets vary from $15 to $20, depending on conditions. Snowmaking equipment enhances Mother Nature's efforts in dry years.

When the slopes close, take a 10-minute walk through the semi–ghost-town of Marysville, and stop at the Marysville House for a libation and an excellent dinner. If you prefer to eat in Helena, head downtown for the best fare: the Windbag Saloon & Grill, the Stonehouse, or On Broadway. The tiny Bistro, a renovated home located next to the ballpark on Lyndale Avenue, serves excellent, eclectic cuisine.

Cross-country skiers generally head up MacDonald Pass and ski the groomed trails near Frontier Town, or create their own trails on public lands atop the pass. If it's a low-snow year and Mount Helena trails are clear, you can hike to the top for a dynamite view of the city and surroundings. Bring good windproof clothes for the summit—no matter how hot you get climbing up, it's a sure bet you'll encounter blustery weather at the top.

Helena has a number of bed and breakfast establishments housed in historic homes. You can't go wrong at any of them. History and antiquing are definite attractions in this gold-rush–era community. Enjoy both by visiting the Original Governor's Mansion, open for tours on the hour from noon to 4 p.m. Tuesdays through Saturdays.

ALONG THE MISSOURI

If Helena didn't take up your entire weekend, drive north on Interstate 15. Look for the Sleeping Giant on the horizon—he's on his back, with a distinct profile and a barrel chest. Keep your eyes open for pronghorn antelope on the flats as I-15 takes you right by the giant's face. Gates of the Mountains Wilderness is just east of the giant.

If the roads are clear and dry, get off the interstate near the head of Little Prickly Pear Creek Canyon and drive the Frontage Road all the way to Ulm. You'll parallel the Mighty Mo, and the slower pace provides up-close-and-personal views of intriguing geology. The red and green layers south of Wolf Creek are mudstones from the Precambrian era; north of Wolf Creek you'll see interlayered lava and ash in the Adel Mountains, the remains of a 50-million-year-old volcano.

Just five miles from Wolf Creek, Holter Lake is a favorite spot for ice fishing. The Missouri doesn't freeze solid below Holter, so hardy anglers often throw a line in. I've floated it every month of the year and can say that there's nothing quite like being on a river in December—the cold winds and bright sunshine add extra flavor to a Thermos of hot chocolate.

Once you are out of the canyon, notice Square Butte rising to the west of the highway. The smaller butte southwest of it is Crown Butte, a Nature Conservancy preserve that protects the unique prairie ecosystem atop the butte.

GREAT FALLS

Great Falls is about 90 miles north of Helena. Here, too, are interesting museums and displays, as well as outdoor attractions. Best-known is the C.M. Russell Museum, which houses the largest collection of paintings by Montana's favorite son. The Trigg Collection downstairs pulls in viewers with glimpses of the warm and personable Charlie Russell. On a 1915 Christmas card painting of a hunter bringing a

ON THE FRONTAGE ROAD, YOU PARALLEL THE MIGHTY MO, UP CLOSE TO INTRIGUING GEOLOGY

deer to a cabin, entitled "Christmas Meat," Russell wrote,

When and where I meet her my hats off to the sow
But I couldent be respectful to that fat old lady now
Tho Im tierd and Wolfish hungry from my long steep mountian tramp
Sowbrest holds no charmes for me when theres
Black tail meat in camp.

Paris Gibson Square, a renovated school, is a museum and cultural center for Great Falls. Volunteers decorate the square for the holidays in time for the annual Christmas Collection in November. This is a juried art show, and holiday shoppers can select from art, food, and crafts, then refortify with an excellent gourmet luncheon (Tuesdays through Fridays) at the Museum Cafe. Other displays include both contemporary and historic exhibitions, as well as the intriguing outdoor sculpture "Gibson Gateway." Paris Gibson founded Great Falls, and this cultural center is a tribute to his foresight.

In addition to the usual motels, there are several bed and breakfasts in Great Falls. The pink and white Sarah is probably the best-known. The proprietors are a wealth of information and good humor.

Downtown Great Falls' Christmas Stroll is held on December 1, from 5:30 to 9:30 p.m. Activities for all ages include street hockey, free horse-drawn wagon rides, singalongs, local entertainment, street vendors, ethnic food booths, and a Santa's village. The decorations and lights downtown add a beautiful touch to this pleasant evening.

Beef fans patronize the Bar S or head for campfire steaks at Eddie's Supper Club at the east end of town.

To put a blush in your cheeks, drive along the Missouri to Giant Springs Heritage State Park. The park is open 8 a.m. to 5 p.m. Monday through Friday all winter, and you can sled on the hills, see the trout hatchery, and watch the water flow. Giant Springs is one

A successful day of ice fishing for Nathan Nelson
JEFF NELSON PHOTO

of the world's largest freshwater springs. Its waters, called the Roe River, flow 201 feet before joining the Missouri, thus making it the world's shortest river.

A number of hydroelectric dams impound the Missouri near Great Falls. When Rainbow Falls Dam was built, someone had the foresight to decree that its backwaters could not flood Giant Springs. It's a shame no one was around to defend the historic, splendid Great Falls of the Missouri, now covered by Ryan Dam.

Malmstrom Air Force Base's museum is staffed by volunteers, and well worth your time. (You must bring a picture identification to the main entrance to gain admittance to the museum.) The outdoors area displays historically important aircraft and vehicles, such as the F-89J Scorpion, KC-97G Stratotanker, LGM-30G Minuteman Missile, and UH-1F Iroquois. Indoor exhibits are open from noon to 3 p.m. on Mondays, Wednesdays, and Fridays throughout the winter. Many Montanans who live with the daily knowledge of Minuteman missiles in our midst report a kind of horrified fascination at seeing the cutaway display of the silos. Montana's 200 Minuteman launch facilities are connected by underground cable to 20 launch control centers. It's mind-boggling to think of the thousands of miles of buried cable that serve each Minuteman squadron.

HEADING SOUTH

Take U.S. Highway 89 south out of Great Falls. If you're ready for lunch, detour south on Highway 227 to the American Bar in Stockett. Pat Merva or one of his family will build—and I mean build—a sandwich you can't get your mouth around without first squashing the sandwich. Vegetarians better go elsewhere, but carnivores will find classic eating for

$4: meat piled as thick as my forefinger is long, between two slices of Eddy's white bread. Various condiments of your choice and a touch of lettuce and tomato finish the package. It's a deal and a half.

If the roads are dry, continue south of Stockett for a few miles, then take the first major left turn onto the Evans-Riceville Road. About 21 miles of this bumpy road brings you through absolutely lovely countryside, with views of the Highwoods and the Little Belts, then back out onto Highway 89 north of Monarch. Don't chance it if the roads are not clear and dry.

If you stayed on Highway 89 and didn't sidetrack to Stockett, you'll find the Black Diamond Supper Club about 20 miles east of Great Falls, in Belt. They offer a large variety of beers and serve decent dinners. It's worth the drive just to eat the poppyseed cake drenched in warm beer butter sauce. Take a walk around town after dinner to see the old jail and historic buildings. In the 1890s, Belt had 1,000 workers employed by the Anaconda Copper Mining Company to mine coal and work the coke ovens. Mining declined and agriculture filled in some of the gaps.

Belt may appear sleepy, but it has had its share of excitement. Belt Creek's big flood in 1953 sent water four feet deep over the highway on the east side of town, and more than half of Belt's 900 residents had to evacuate. You can get a closer view of Belt Creek from the swinging bridge near the jail. It's a handy shortcut for locals, but don't cross it if you tend to get vertigo.

Another of Belt's claim-to-fame disasters occurred in the winter of 1976, when a freight train jumped the tracks and ruptured fuel storage tanks. Burning oil and fuel ran down the street towards the

The Sleeping Giant
JOHN LAMBING PHOTO

business district, and one explosion threw a fireball 1,000 feet in the air.

SKI & SOAK

Showdown Ski Area is a treat. There are 34 runs on this unassuming mountain, and the snow is reliable. Many winters I've driven there through a totally snowless landscape wondering how in the world a ski area could survive here, only to arrive at Showdown and find perfect conditions. They have a death-defying back side for experts only, and the many beginner and intermediate slopes are perfect for learning to telemark or snowboard.

You can't overnight at the ski area, but there are a few motels in nearby Neihart and Monarch. White Sulphur Springs has several bed and breakfasts, as well as the Spa Motel and its outdoor hot-

springs pool. Everyone should treat themselves to its relaxing mineral waters in midwinter. The prominent stone mansion in town is The Castle, now housing the Meagher County Historical Association's exhibits, open in he summer.

About nine miles south of White Sulphur, turn west on U.S. Highway 12. The road climbs Grassy Mountain before dropping into Deep Creek. On either side of the highway, cross-country skiers will find numerous jump-off points for skiing old roads into the Helena National Forest. Farther down the canyon, the Deep Creek Restaurant serves very good dinners in its lovely log building beside the creek.

In winter, Townsend volunteers operate the Broadwater County Museum by appointment only. If you're here the first weekend of

December, it will seem the whole town is part of the Townsend Christmas Stroll. Ice-boaters and skaters have a field day at Canyon Ferry. Given the right conditions, which is usually the case, you can zip around atop miles of the frozen surface. Skate sailers, tots being towed on sleds, hot-shot iceboat racers, ice fishers, and recreational skaters all share the ice and the camaraderie. The Silos area usually has the best ice conditions—Canyon Ferry in winter is definitely one of Montana's premier outdoor recreation attractions.

Driving back to Helena completes the loop for this south-central Montana gem. ✧

Ski, Sip, Sup, and Soak

by Duncan Adams

Bozeman's Main Street can turn you on or turn your stomach, depending upon your take on the New West. The old cow town has gone trendy, with cappuccino bars, art galleries, and pricey boutiques. Sensitive, New-Age Guys (SNAGs) clad in Patagonia parkas tote babies in Kelty backpacks while lithe women stride about armed with ski poles and Evian bottles.

For some, such sights stir a deep yearning for even a fleeting glimpse of a wizened, gimpy cowpoke with cowflop on his boots.

There are at least two possible courses of action in Bozeman. One—go ahead and indulge: quaff a memorable cup of coffee at the Leaf and Bean; consume a unique pizza at Mackenzie River Pizza Company; browse the impressive inventory at the Country Bookshelf—all on Main Street. Shop at Northern Lights Trading Company for high-tech longjohns that could wick dry a banana and break a Rockefeller; enjoy a massage from a therapist at Alpenglow. Consider a visit to the Museum of the Rockies, home to dinosaur exhibits and other wonders. Ponder downhill skiing at unpretentious Bridger Bowl or nordic skiing at Bohart Ranch, both just a 20-minute drive north

Cross-country skier in Yellowstone National Park
ERWIN C. "BUD" NIELSEN PHOTO

of town. If you need a good pair of winter boots (or feel kinship to Imelda Marcos) stop at Schnee's Boots and Shoes at 121 West Main.

Or, two—quiet your riotous wintry longing in quintessential American fashion, with a road trip. The 215-mile route described here—Bozeman to West Yellowstone to Ennis and back—appeals to aesthete, athlete, and hedonist alike. It is, by and large, a river route, following the sinuous, scenic, and seismically active contours of the Gallatin and Madison rivers.

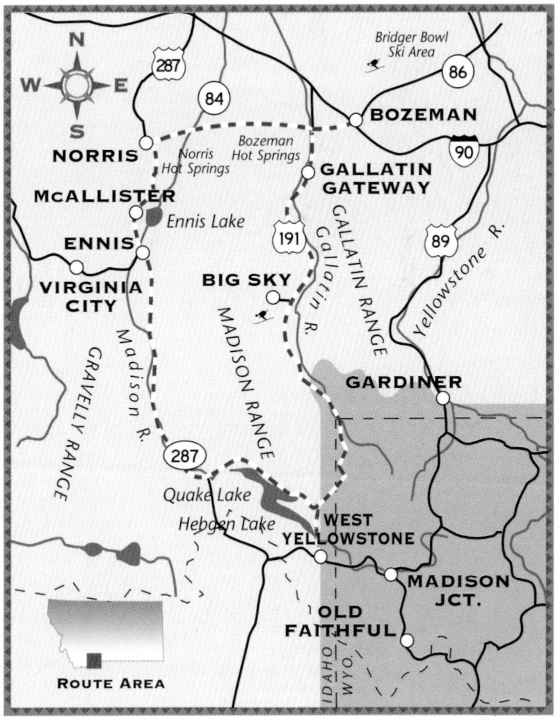

GALLATIN GATEWAY AND CANYON

From Bozeman, drive west approximately six miles on High-

way 191 until you reach its intersection with highways 84 and 85. Here, at this four-way stop, Highway 191 turns left toward Big Sky and West Yellowstone. You should, too. A short mile down the road Bozeman Hot Springs

101

Big Sky Resort
RICK & SUSIE GRAETZ PHOTO

offers indoor swimming in natural hot springs pools. Winter's pasty-white bathers can play in the big, warm pool, turn lobster-red in one of the hot pools, and finish off blue after an icy plunge.

Five miles later, watch for the historic Gallatin Gateway Inn, a fine and charming place to lodge, dine, or simply dawdle for backside warming near the great fireplace. Built by the Chicago, Milwaukee and St. Paul Railway, the inn opened in 1927. This grand hotel, originally designed to serve railroad passengers bound ultimately by bus for Yellowstone National Park, offers a striking example of Spanish Colonial Revival architecture. It is listed on the National Register of Historic Places.

Seven miles past the Gallatin Gateway Inn, Highway 191 enters the mouth of the Gallatin River Canyon. The Shoshone Indians called the green, rolling river that cut the canyon the *Cut-tuh-o-gwa,* meaning "Swift Water." Meriwether Lewis and William Clark were less poetic. They named it for President Thomas Jefferson's treasury secretary, Albert Gallatin.

It is one of Montana's most celebrated trout streams. Anglers ply its unfrozen sections even in the heart of winter. Gallatin Riverguides, based in Big Sky, offers half-day guided fishing trips during the winter months. "The fishing is more consistent in February and March than in January," said guide Tom Vetter.

The Gallatin Range of the

Rockies rises to the east of the north-south canyon, the Madison Range to the west. The craggy Spanish Peaks are west of Highway 191 at the canyon's northern end. Backcountry skiers can watch for Spanish Creek Road, which joins Highway 191 approximately two miles into the canyon. The gravel county road usually is passable at its start, but by January, snowdrifts typically block vehicle access to the last three and a half miles before the trailhead. Skiers simply park and ski. The Spanish Creek Trail enters the Spanish Peaks Unit of the Lee Metcalf Wilderness. Skiers can reserve the nearby Spanish Creek recreation cabin by calling the Bozeman Ranger District at 587-6920. Check avalanche conditions (587-6981) before proceeding into the high country. The Bozeman Ranger District provides information about other cross-country skiing opportunities and an extensive network of area snowmobile trails, including the 123-mile-long Big Sky Snowmobile Trail.

Continuing south on 191, note Sheep Rock and Castle Rock, limestone cliffs carved by wind, water, and time.

BIG SKY

Forty-one miles from Bozeman you'll encounter the entrance to the Big Sky Ski and Summer Resort, owned and operated by Boyne USA Inc. Both aesthete and hedonist should pause at Moose Rack Books in the Bighorn Center on Highway 191. Peruse the store's new and rare books. Savor an espresso and a pastry.

Gallatin Gourmet Deli, two miles up the Big Sky road in the Meadow Village, is a good choice for lunch, especially for those on the move. Big Sky offers a variety of dining, lodging, and shopping opportunities. (Phone 800-548-4486 for an information package.) Athletes may decide to proceed directly to Big Sky's downhill ski area, dreamchild of the late Chet Huntley. In November 1994, *The New York Times* reported that the variety of trails at Big Sky would "keep all but the most die-hard skiers interested for five days."

The resort's new Lone Peak Tram transports skiers (and non-skiers) to the 11,166-foot summit of Lone Peak. On a clear day, you can see almost forever. Big Sky offers a variety of family-oriented

services. Two children 10-and-under can ski free with each paying adult. The resort prides itself on short lift lines. Nordic skiers should stop at Lone Mountain Ranch, described by *Cross Country Skier* magazine as a "cross-country skier's paradise." The ranch offers 75 kilometers of professionally groomed ski trails over a variety of terrain. Full-day and half-day ski passes are reasonably priced and rental equipment is available. Kids 12-and-under ski free. Typically, January and February feature good to excellent skiing conditions,

with January noted for deep powder. Lone Mountain Ranch offers also an "old fashioned sleigh ride dinner." Diners board a horse-drawn sleigh for a 20-minute ride through the woods to a quaint cabin. There, a chef prepares dinner over a wood-burning cookstove. (Call 995-2783 for reservations.)

YELLOWSTONE FLIRTATION

Once fully satiated on Big Sky's buzz, continue south on Highway 191. You'll soon encounter Buck's

Old Faithful in Yellowstone Park
JEFF & ALEXA HENRY PHOTO

T-4 Lodge, a Best Western motel wrapped around an old hunting camp built in 1946 by Buck and Helen Knight. The motel offers perhaps the area's most reasonable room rates during the height of ski season. And *The New York Times* described dinner at Buck's T-4 Dining Room as "a pleasant surprise," featuring wild game entrees "beautifully prepared with light sauces." Hungry travelers also stop at the Corral Bar and Cafe—approximately five miles south of Big Sky—renowned for huge, juicy hamburgers. Twelve miles south of Big Sky, watch for the 320 Guest Ranch, which offers

fine dining, lodging, sleigh rides, and a variety of other services. The ranch, first homesteaded by Sam and Josie Wilson in 1899 as the Buffalo Horn Ranch, is one of Gallatin Canyon's historic dude ranches.

The Gallatin Canyon begins to open up and rolling hills replace steep rock walls. During the fall of 1886, "Buckskin Charley" Marble guided future president Teddy Roosevelt on a 40-day hunting trip in the area, traveling up Sage Creek and Taylor's Fork, and beyond.

Shortly after leaving the canyon's embrace, motorists enter

the northwest corner of Yellowstone National Park. There is no entrance station here, just a sign. This brief flirtation with the park offers some backcountry ski trails, glimpses of the effects of the fires of 1988, and occasional sightings of bison, elk, and other weighty mammals, but provides no encounters with Yellowstone's most famous geologic features. For such contact, travelers must bundle up and strap on skis, straddle

Mist and snow on the Firehole River
RICK & SUSIE GRAETZ PHOTO

snowmobiles, or hunker down in rumbling snowcoaches. West Yellowstone is a good place to start.

WEST YELLOWSTONE

Approximately 20 miles after entering Yellowstone National Park's northwest corner, you'll leave it and re-enter the Gallatin National Forest. At Grayling Creek, the road climbs to the crest of a hill, opening a panoramic view of the Yellowstone Plateau, described in *Roadside Geology of Montana* as "the edge of one of the biggest active volcanoes in the world." At the center of Yellowstone National Park is a giant volcano called a "resurgent caldera." According to authors David Alt and Donald W. Hyndman, Yellowstone's caldera is just about due (give or take a few thousand years) for another big blow: "The Yellowstone resurgent caldera has gone through at least three major eruptions at intervals of approximately 600,000 years, the last about that long ago."

These eruptive probabilities are best contemplated over a steaming cup of java. A good place in West Yellowstone for such ruination rumination is the Book Peddler on Canyon Street, which houses Cappy's Coffee Bar.

In summer, West Yellowstone

RENDEZVOUS SKI TRAIL FROM WEST YELLOWSTONE IS ONE OF THE AREA'S SKIER-ONLY TRAILS

thrums with tourists. In winter, snowmobilers rule. The town calls itself the "Snowmobile Capital of the World," and it's easy to understand why. The machines rumble and fume, buzzing the streets and trails. More than 1,000 miles of snowmobile trails fan out from town.

Many snowmobilers favor forays into Yellowstone National Park. Consult park regulations and season dates. A dozen or more area businesses offer snowmobile rentals—check with the Yellowstone Chamber of Commerce at 646-7701 for details and call in advance to reserve machines.

Nordic skiers need not despair of having to breathe gas fumes all day. There are skier-only routes in the area, such as the Rendezvous Ski Trail, which originates right in West Yellowstone, offering more than 30 kilometers of professionally-groomed trails.

Others destined for winter visits into Yellowstone National Park rely on heated, enclosed

West Yellowstone: Snowmobile capital of the world
RICK & SUSIE GRAETZ PHOTO

snowcoaches, which can be chartered from West Yellowstone.

Fine cuisine does not rate high among West Yellowstone's claims to fame. It's easier to find a "Bear Whiz" tee-shirt in this often-gaudy gateway town than a memorable meal. But there are restaurants worth mentioning: Three Bear Restaurant on Yellowstone Avenue serves breakfast and dinner; Stage Coach Inn features a coffee shop and dining room; Silver Spur offers traditional, inexpensive fare and frequently serves up a hearty soup. A number of shops remain open during the winter, poised and ready to take your money. Shopping opportunities range from tacky to tasteful.

Motels dominate the lodging scene. The Stage Coach Inn is a full-service hotel. Reservations are recommended during the busy snowmobile season.

QUAKE LAKE

Backtrack out of West Yellowstone and head north on Highway 287. Travel approximately eight miles to the junction with Highway 191 and turn west, staying on Highway 287, toward Ennis. The road hugs Hebgen Lake's north shore. A local guide admitted that ice-fishing can be good on the lake, but added that he's no fan of this eccentric cousin to fly fishing: "I'd rather go out in the woods and poke myself in the eye with a sharp stick."

The Madison River Canyon earthquake area is truly astounding to contemplate. At 11:37 p.m. on August 17, 1959, several area faults shifted simultaneously. These shifts triggered a violent earthquake that measured 7.5 on the Richter scale, setting off a massive landslide in the Madison Canyon. The slide completely blocked the Madison River, creating Quake Lake. Twenty-eight people perished, buried under debris and boulders, or drowned when a wall of water swept through the Rock Creek Campground. Hebgen Lake's earth-filled dam, completed in 1915, cracked but held fast. A drive through the earthquake area is a fascinating and sobering experience, offering tangible evidence both of the earth's power and its ongoing transformation. The visitor center at Quake Lake is closed in the winter.

ENNIS

Leaving the Madison Canyon, the road enters the broad southern end of the Madison River valley. Highway 287 dogs the river for 40-plus miles to the town of Ennis. To the east, flatlands and benches extend to the foothills of the dramatic Madison Range. Pronghorn antelope and mule deer graze the benches while raptors soar and perch. Winter is quiet in Ennis, which bustles in summer with tourists bound for Yellowstone and anglers bound for the river.

IN A FEW VIOLENT MINUTES OF AUGUST 1959, QUAKE LAKE WAS BORN

The town's most famous restaurant, The Continental Divide, is closed in winter. The Ennis Cafe offers standard small-town Montana fare. The Yesterday restaurant, housed in the Ennis Pharmacy, serves breakfast and lunch and features old-fashioned soda-fountain concoctions made with Wilcoxson's ice cream. The Hole in the Wall Gallery deserves a browse.

North of Ennis the highway must leave the Madison River, which enters the narrow whitewater gorge of the Beartrap Canyon. At McAllister, some seven miles from Ennis, the Bear Claw Bar & Grill, formerly the McAllister Inn, serves lunch and dinner and is a favorite of many locals.

Nine miles from Ennis, 287 begins a long climb. Specialized fences block drifts, but blowing snow can make the hill north of McAllister a drive requiring concentration. At the hill's crest, a marker describes traces of the Bozeman Trail still visible (when not snow-covered). The trail, laid out in 1863 by John Bozeman and John Jacobs, provided a cutoff from the Oregon Trail into the gold-rush towns of southwest Montana.

Looking across the Madison Valley to the Madison Range
RICK & SUSIE GRAETZ PHOTO

Norris Hot Springs
SCOTT WHEELER PHOTO

NORRIS

Norris is situated at the junction of highways 287 and 84. Bear right on 84 toward Bozeman about a mile and stop at Bear Trap Hot Springs. It's nothing fancy, but the pool is hot (between 104 and 106 degrees), the beer cold, the price right, and the clientele varied. On a recent visit, beer-bellied older men slugged brews, a young couple nuzzled in a corner, and some children dove and splashed. With some exceptions, Bear Trap Hot Springs is open year-round 11 a.m. to 11 p.m.

Sunday through Thursday and 10:30 a.m. to midnight Friday and Saturday.

Approximately three miles east of Norris, you'll pass the Red Bluff Research Ranch of Montana State University, once the site of the town of Red Bluff. "During the 1880s and 1890s, Red Bluff became an important stage stop on the road connecting Bozeman and Virginia City," according to *A Traveler's Companion to Montana History*. Today, a handsome two-story stone building, circa mid-1960s, remains from that early settlement.

Five more miles brings a brief and scenic reunion with the

Madison River after it emerges from Beartrap Canyon, a busy recreational area during spring, summer and fall. The loop is completed when you rejoin Highway 191 west of Bozeman.

A RIVER ROUTE

Norman Maclean wrote, "I am haunted by waters." The waters along this route certainly work their spell—brave an exit from your warm vehicle and pause to listen to the melody of the Madison, or stop to peer into the Gallatin's green depths. These waters have miles to travel across the continent. And you are almost home. ✧

INDEX

INDEX

INDEX

$15.95

THE BEST OF
MONTANA
MAGAZINE

FOUR-SEASON TRAVEL

FIFTEEN TOWN-AND-COUNTRY LOOP TRIPS TAKE YOU ALL AROUND
MONTANA, IN ALL FOUR SEASONS. THE AUTHORS INCLUDE INFORMATION ON
RECREATION OPPORTUNITIES AND LOCAL EVENTS YOU WON'T WANT TO MISS.
GET THE BEST INSIDERS' SUGGESTIONS ON RESTAURANTS, SHOPPING,
FESTIVALS, HIDDEN PARKS, ROAD AND WEATHER SITUATIONS, AND MUCH
MORE. FULL-COLOR MAPS AND PHOTOGRAPHS ENHANCE THIS COLLECTION
GATHERED FROM THE POPULAR SERIES IN MONTANA MAGAZINE.

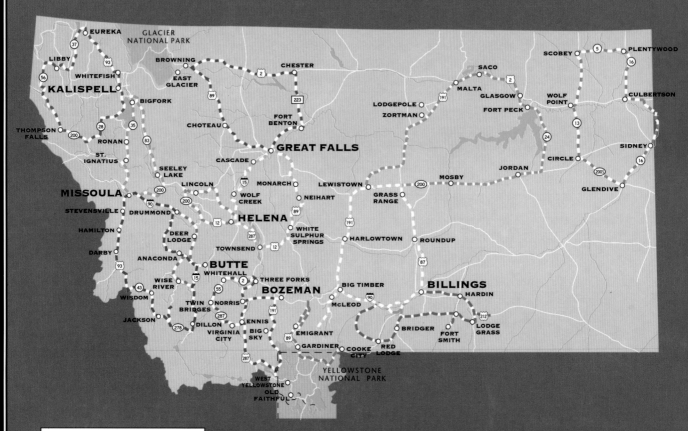

ISBN 1-56037-136-6
51595

9 781560 371366